THE LIGHT OF OPTIMISM

The Autobiography of
Trilok Raj Sharma, PhD
with Sangita Sharma

THE LIGHT OF OPTIMISM
Accepting Life As It Comes

The Autobiography of
TRILOK RAJ SHARMA, PhD
with Sangita Sharma

NewDelhi • London

BLUEROSE PUBLISHERS
India | U.K.

Copyright © Dr Trilok Raj Sharma, Dr Sangita Sharma 2024

All rights reserved by author. No part of this publication may be reproduced, stored in a retrieval system or transmitted in any form or by any means, electronic, mechanical, photocopying, recording or otherwise, without the prior permission of the author. Although every precaution has been taken to verify the accuracy of the information contained herein, the publisher assumes no responsibility for any errors or omissions. No liability is assumed for damages that may result from the use of information contained within.

BlueRose Publishers takes no responsibility for any damages, losses, or liabilities that may arise from the use or misuse of the information, products, or services provided in this publication.

For permissions requests or inquiries regarding this publication,
please contact:

BLUEROSE PUBLISHERS
www.BlueRoseONE.com
info@bluerosepublishers.com
+91 8882 898 898
+4407342408967

Contact Author: +91 9549500137

ISBN: 978-93-6452-141-3

Cover design: Shivani
Typesetting: Sagar

First Edition: October 2024

"In these frames lie the colours of my life, woven into the fabric of time, each picture a reminder that it's the journey, not the destination, that truly matters!"

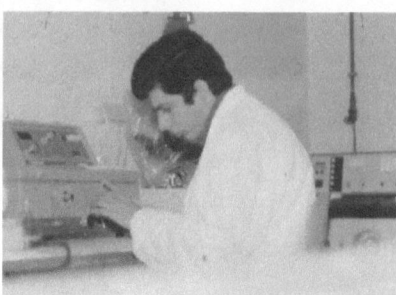

Dedication

Dedicated

to
My most respected

Parents

and

Teachers

(Professional and Spiritual)

Acknowledgements

I am immensely grateful to my wife, Krishna, who has stood by me through thick and thin throughout my life. I am also grateful to my elder son-in-law, Dr. Vaibhav Vaishnav, for his recent support during my hospitalisation and treatment in critical condition. His help has been invaluable during this challenging time.

I am thankful to my daughters, Dr. Sangita and Er. Gunjan, who have given me moral support in difficult times. Their presence is a source of bliss in our lives. I will always remain grateful to my only son, late Ankur Sharma, for his sincerity and dedication towards me and my wife throughout his life. I will always cherish the joy and happiness he brought into our lives.

I am also grateful to all my extended family members, both younger and older, especially my brothers, late Mr. Mahesh, Mr. Kailash, and Dr. Subhash, with whom I share a special bond and many cherished memories. Special thanks to my soul sister, whose love and affection have lasted for more than 65 years.

I also express my gratitude to my childhood friends, namely, the late Ratan Lal Koli, Jugal Kishore Poddar, and Kamlesh Kanak, for the beautiful moments we spent together during our carefree yet formative childhood days.

I will always remember the great help rendered by my friend, Mr. Gauri Shankar Paliwal, and his family during my stay in Udaipur.

In Delhi, I cannot forget the bond I developed with Dr. Sheo Prakash Shukla, to the extent that we were fondly called 'Laxmikant Pyarelal' by our hostel mates.

In West Germany, my sincere thanks go to Marianne, who also came to India with her mother to witness my marriage ceremony, which interested them. My life was made easier because of my teacher Dr. Avtar Krishna Kaul and his family, who called me from Delhi to Germany, opening further opportunities for me. I will always remain grateful to them. Germans, in general, are very friendly and supportive, and I will always remember and be thankful to many of them.

In Nigeria, the atmosphere and life, in general, were entirely different from Germany. However, our ten-year stay was pleasant and without much trouble. In fact, some of the fondest memories of my children are from Nigeria.

Back in India, my service and postings in Fatehpur Shekhawati and later in Bikaner were pleasant, though I lived alone most of the time. In both places, people were nice to me. I vividly remember Dr. Prithvi Singh, Dr. Vishal Singh, and Dr. Aman Rustagi, who were veterinary students and have been respectful to me as their teacher.

After retirement, I have been living in Jaipur with my joint family for the last 17 years, happily and content amidst all the ebbs and flows of life. This has been possible by joining and rigorously practising Vipassana meditation. In this endeavour, I am grateful to Mr. Ashok Chauhan for introducing me to Vipassana and Shri Anil Mehtaji, a Vipassana teacher at Dhamma Thali Jaipur Centre, who has been of great help in strengthening my Vipassana meditation. It has changed my life entirely and has given me tremendous strength, especially through life's ups and downs.

I may have forgotten to mention all my friends and relatives who have contributed to my welfare and well-being, but I am thankful to each one of them.

I would be remiss if I did not mention my elder daughter, Dr. Sangita, who conceived the idea of penning down the story of my life. This idea, which was in its infancy, developed into a firm determination, and finally, my daughter embarked on writing the detailed life sketch into an autobiography. I am very happy and thankful to her for this endeavour.

This autobiography is not merely a chronicle of events but a testament to the human spirit's capacity to endure, evolve and ultimately find meaning in the tapestry of existence. It is my fervent hope that my story resonates with readers from all walks of life, offering encouragement, reflection and a profound reminder that amidst life's trials, there exists boundless potential for growth, healing, and the pursuit of happiness.

Dr. Trilok Raj Sharma
MSc, PhD

Preface

I have been fortunate enough to be one of the closest people in Dr. Trilok Raj Sharma's life, being his first child. However, this is not the only reason I attempted to pen down the journey of his life in his own words. The tapestry of his life has been a narrative woven with threads of joy, resilience, profound loss, and unwavering hope. He is a man of a unique combination of great perseverance and determination on one hand, and extreme resilience, compassion, and contentment on the other.

Being his firstborn child, I have been a part of his life for the last 45 years, as I turn 45 today. I have witnessed some major triumphs and trials in his life, and the way he navigated through them is an inspiration for everyone. Besides, he is a wonderful storyteller too. He often reminisces and narrates incidents from his life, both from his yesteryears and everyday routine. He has the ability to make every narration interesting, full of wit and humour, yet very inspiring, with a lesson of life ingrained in it. I have seen people of all age groups, including his grandchildren, being deeply engaged in his stories.

I realised that individuals from all walks of life would relate to this story and hopefully proceed with inspiration and more enthusiasm on their respective paths. His journey from the humble beginnings of a modest family to the corridors of premier research institutions in India and later international universities in Germany and Nigeria will be a great source of inspiration for aspiring students struggling to fulfil their dreams amidst life's challenges.

This is a tale of a common man. It will fascinate everyone, whether a young enthusiast full of life, a dreamer, an achiever, a young scientist facing different scenarios in India and the Western world or people willing to return to their motherland after spending a long time abroad. It will evoke interest in youngsters who love to travel and explore different places and cultures. It will resonate with fathers who try their best and contribute significantly to their children's crucial phases of life despite challenging professional commitments and with those who have faced the loss of their dear ones and emerged stronger with the memories left behind. It will give strength to people struggling with serious health issues like cancer. Finally this story will reverberate with those who have found their peace and strength on the path of meditation, and all those who have embraced the different colours of life with a sense of fulfilment, gratitude and contentment.

I had been thinking of writing his story for a long time, but in the hustle and bustle of life, I could not gather the courage to initiate it. Recently, two incidents pushed me into making serious efforts for this book. The first was the decluttering of the almirahs and cupboards in my parents' house, where I found them disposing of some old letters, photographs, souvenirs, and academic material like certificates and research papers. Each had a great story and memories attached to it, whether it be the memory of challenges faced, accomplishments, success, joy, companionship, perseverance or contentment.

As I saw my parents wrap up significant phases of their lives and comfortably decide to discard these things, which had been of great value at some point in their lifetime, I learned the lesson of adapting to the flow of life. The lesson of giving the best of yourself in every endeavour and phase, yet being content, knowing when to slow down. This story would inspire the youth to dream big and believe that with vision, perseverance, and humility, any dream can become a reality. I learned the importance of enriching experiences, building relationships and bonds, and being remembered as a helping hand rather than being attached to materialistic things, whose value fades with time. I thought of preserving all these beautiful memories in the form of a collection of interesting stories, giving it the shape of a book.

The second reason that prompted me to pen down his journey was his recently diagnosed medical illness. The courage and calm with which he faced the situation proved that one can still choose to dissociate physical illness and suffering from mental suffering. Despite the illness and pain inflicted on your body, you have a choice to believe that you are not a victim or a sufferer at heart. This strength came from his long journey of Vipassana meditation and introspection.

Most of the narrations given by him were during his second radiation therapy, which involved whole-brain irradiation. The doctors said he could become dull and drowsy and might develop forgetfulness. But his immense and unmatched inner strength and willpower encouraged me to proceed with the narrations and recordings. In the mornings and forenoons, he would spend around two hours narrating his recollections and stories, and in the evenings, from 4-6 pm, he would attend the radiation therapy sessions.

I consider myself blessed to be a part of the whole process of bringing this book into shape. Listening to Dr. Trilok Raj Sharma for hours, as he re-lived every experience of his life, this time with more wisdom, clarity, and contentment, has been equivalent to a spiritual journey for me.

I hope whoever reads this life history enjoys the twists and turns, feels the positivity and optimism instilled not only in the story but also in the whole process of the narrations and writing, and emerges stronger, happier, and more peaceful in the end, which is the whole purpose of it.

The lessons I learnt from him:

*'Simplicity Shines, Optimism Leads
and Determination Conquers'*

**Dr. Sangita Sharma
MBBS, MD, FNB**

Contents

Dedication	ix
Acknowledgements	xi
Preface	xv

Chapter 1
From Modest Beginnings — 1

Chapter 2
The Harvest of Hard Work — 9

Chapter 3
Nurtured by a Visionary: Journey with Legendary Dr M.S. Swaminathan — 25

Chapter 4
An Energetic Soul Captivated by Movies, Music, and Literature — 45

Chapter 5
Green Revolution to World Class Research: Post Doctoral Pursuits in Germany — 51

Chapter 6
Homecoming and the Harmonious Arranged Union — 71

Chapter 7
Together in Deutschland: Journey Back to Germany with Better Half — 81

Chapter 8
A Joyous Return: Homecoming with Gifts & Tokens of Affection — 93

Chapter 9
   Partners in Adventure: Into Nigeria
   and the Heart of Africa   99

Chapter 10
   Wanderlust Chronicles: Eagerness to
   Explore Cultures and Countries   133

Chapter 11
   Krishna, My Dear Wife: The Backbone of My Life   155

Chapter 12
   Sowing New Beginnings: Defying
   Stereotypes in Agriculture   165

Chapter 13
   A Transformative Tenure at the Agricultural
   Research Station, Fatehpur-Shekhawati   169

Chapter 14
   A Brief and Impactful Stint at the
   Directorate of Research   181

Chapter 15
   The Circle of Belonging: The Tree
   of Modern Joint Family   191

Chapter 16
   Our Elder Daughter: The Pride of Our Family   211

Chapter 17
   Our Son: An Inspiring Tale of Dedication and Grit   219

Chapter 18
   Our Younger Daughter: A Story of
   Growth and Success   237

Chapter 19
   The Heartbreaking Loss of Our Son
   and the Aftermath   243

Chapter 20
    From Chaos to Clarity: Spiritual Metamorphosis
    with Vipassana   251

Chapter 21
    Defying the Odds: My Relentless
    Fight Against Cancer   265

Chapter 22
    Dreams Unfolding: The Art of Finding
    Contentment and Peace in Simplicity   279

Epilogue
    Reflections of a Life Lived with
    Optimism and Resilience   283

Chapter 1

From Modest Beginnings

My story begins with the simplicity and contentment that marked my early life. I was born to Shri Mangi Lalji Sharma and Smt Champa Devi Sharma, on a crisp autumn day, the 5th of October, 1948, in the vibrant and historic city of Jaipur, the Pink City. It was the *'Teej'* (third day) of the auspicious *Sharad Navratri*. Official records, however, list my date of birth as 10th March, 1947, a reflection of the casual record-keeping practices of that era.

Our family was large and lively, consisting of seven siblings, four brothers and three sisters. My father was the sole breadwinner, working tirelessly to support us. Despite our limited financial resources, our home was rich in love and joy, making our modest household feel abundant.

> *"In the humblest of beginnings lies the foundation of resilience and gratitude."*

During my entire school education, we lived in a rented house lacking basic amenities such as water and electricity. Our evenings were illuminated by a kerosene lamp, and we relied on a public tap for bathing and washing. Despite

Plate 1
My parents, 'Kakaji' and 'Amma', sometime after their marriage. **Shri Mangilalji Sharma**, *my father, was a man with unwavering determination, honesty and simplicity.*
Smt Champa Devi Sharma, *my mother was a great source of strength and love*

Plate 2
Myself as a teenager, 1965

Plate 3a
My Elder Brother: Mahesh Bhaisahab

Plate 3b
My Younger Brother: Kailash

Plate 3c
My Youngest Brother: Subhash

these hardships, we made the best of what we had. These early struggles forged our resilience and resourcefulness. My father imparted invaluable lessons in hard work, determination, and honesty. The sense of togetherness and resilience we shared made those days some of the happiest ones of my life.

Life during my childhood was simple, often spent running around in just shorts and vests. Growing up in a middle-class neighbourhood, our days were filled with laughter and playful games with other children. One of our favourite games was *Sitoliya*, also known as Seven Stones, where we would stack up stones and try to knock them down with a ball. We also played *Gilli Danda* and a hopscotch-like game involving jumping on drawn patterns.

We lived in the heart of Jaipur's old walled city, known as '*Chaar Diwari*.' Despite Jaipur's reputation as a well-planned city, the streets in our area were narrow and congested. My father's shop was about fifty yards from our house, located in the bustling market area near the 'Hawa Mahal'.

I had a deep fear of darkness and being alone. When returning home from tuition classes, I would call out for my mother as soon as I reached the corner of our street, exclaiming, "Amma, come here." The neighbours would wonder about my cries, but I couldn't help it. If anyone walked with me through the alley, I felt braver. Even today, I still have a slight fear of dogs.

> *"The simplicity of childhood reminds us
> that happiness resides in the smallest moments."*

As a child, I was a mediocre student. My early schooling took place in government schools, which, by today's standards, were quite basic. The classrooms were often overcrowded, the facilities sparse, and the resources limited. However, these limitations instilled a sense of camaraderie and shared struggle among my classmates and me. We learned to be creative with our learning, making the best of the resources available to us.

Reflecting on my past, I understand that success is not determined by where you come from but by how you make the best use of what you have.

One of the most memorable times of the year was during the kite festival, *Makar Sankranti*, on 14th January. The excitement for kite flying began months in advance. Winter was perfect for this festival. We would wake up early, rush to the rooftop, and start flying kites. My mother would call us to remind us of the time, urging us to get ready for school or have our meals, but we were too engrossed in our kites. We lived in a two-story house, and the rooftop was our playground. In the evenings, after school, we would return to the rooftop to continue flying kites, often without changing our clothes. These moments were among the fondest of my childhood, filled with simplicity, joy, and carefreeness.

Life in a large family was chaotic yet joyous. We siblings shared everything; clothes, toys, dreams, and aspirations. My brothers and sisters were my first friends and confidants. We played together, studied together, and supported each other through thick and thin. Despite our lack of material wealth, we were rich in love and solidarity. This familial support system played a crucial role in shaping who I am today.

I often marvel at how far I have come from my humble beginnings. It sometimes surprises me, prompting moments of deep introspection. How did I achieve all this?

The answer lies in a combination of destiny, the invaluable lessons from my parents, and the fortune of meeting remarkable people throughout my life. Each mentor, teacher, and friend played a pivotal role in my journey, guiding me through challenges.

My father was one such influential figure. His dedication to his craft, despite meagre earnings, was inspirational. He taught us the importance of hard work, integrity, and resilience. Even after a long day of binding books, he would sit with us, ensuring we did our homework and understood the value of education. His silent sacrifices and unwavering commitment to our well-being were lessons in humility and strength.

My mother was also a pillar of strength. Managing a large household on a tight budget required immense skill and patience. She was resourceful, turning simple ingredients into delicious meals and repurposing old clothes into new garments. Her creativity and ability to maximise limited resources left a lasting impression on me. She taught us that no matter how little we had, there was always a way to make it enough.

Reflecting on my childhood, I am filled with gratitude. The challenges we faced equipped us with the skills to overcome future obstacles. Our upbringing instilled in us a sense of humility and the understanding that true wealth lies in the strength of our character and the relationships we build.

One of the most profound lessons from my early years is the importance of optimism. Despite difficulties, I always carried hope and positivity. This outlook was crucial in navigating the various challenges I encountered, allowing me to see opportunities where others saw obstacles and to believe in a better future.

In these modest beginnings, amidst the warmth of family and the challenges of daily life, my journey began. The values learnt during these formative years guided me through the further chapters of my life, from personal struggles and career achievements to profound losses and triumphs. Through it all, the lessons of my childhood remain a constant source of strength and inspiration.

Chapter 2:

The Harvest of Hard Work

Educational Beginnings

My educational journey began at a government school, where I was an average student. Although I wasn't a standout scholar, I never failed a grade. This consistency instilled in me a quiet confidence, gradually laying the foundation for my future academic pursuits.

From 9th to 11th standard (1961-1964), I attended Raja Ram Dev Poddar Higher Secondary School, a government institution with a vast building and a large ground near the University of Rajasthan. It still stands today on Jawahar Lal Nehru (JLN) Marg, one of Jaipur's prime locations. I had to walk approximately 3-4 kilometres daily from home to school since bicycles were neither common nor easily affordable for us at the time.

In the 9th standard, I opted for science and mathematics, subjects that fascinated me but also demanded a higher level of understanding and dedication. It was during this period that I experienced my first academic failure. The disappointment of not

Plate 4
Raja Ram Dev Poddar School: A cornerstone of education and camaraderie, where my journey of learning truly began through Classes 9 to 11 (1961-64). (Image Source: Facebook page of Poddar School Jaipur)

passing was a harsh wake-up call, a reminder that the path to success is often lined with obstacles. Yet, this setback did not deter me; instead, it fuelled my determination to excel.

Despite this hiccup, I managed to secure first-class marks throughout the rest of my schooling and college life. The board exams in the 11th class were pivotal, marking the culmination of years of hard work and serving as the gateway to higher education. Clearing these exams with commendable marks was a significant achievement, bolstering my confidence as I stepped into the next phase of my academic journey.

I chose to pursue my graduation in Agriculture at the Rajasthan College of Agriculture in Udaipur, part of Sukhadia University. Gaining admission to this esteemed institution was a significant achievement, filling me with pride and hope for the future. During that time, students of engineering and medicine were considered superior, while agriculture was not given much importance. However, a few years later, agriculture gained recognition and respect. This shift in perception was partly due to widespread hunger in India and the country's dependence on food imports.

Prime Minister Mrs. Indira Gandhi often expressed her frustration to agricultural scientists, saying, "I don't want to go abroad with a begging bowl. How long will we continue to beg for food?" Her words underscored the critical importance of agriculture in achieving self-sufficiency for the nation. Soon, the famous and much-needed 'Green Revolution' began taking root in India.

"Education is not just about learning; it's about navigating the twists and turns that shape our journey."

Memories: Lifelong Bonds

Back in my school days in Jaipur, I was fortunate to meet Ratanlal Koli at Raja Ram Dev Poddar Higher Secondary School. Our friendship began when I failed the 9th grade and joined his class, despite being a year ahead. This setback led to a lifelong bond with one of the most remarkable individuals I've ever known.

Ratanlal came from a weaver community in *Kachhi Basti*. Despite his humble background, he consistently topped the class, always securing the first position. His academic brilliance was matched only by his love for reading. He devoured every novel in the public library, often reading them more than once, and rented additional books to quench his thirst for knowledge. Ratanlal was more than just a scholar. He had an insatiable love for movies, never missing a single release, and surprised everyone with his talent for singing and dancing. At parties, he would captivate everyone with his melodious voice and impressive dance moves, a rarity in our circle at the time.

After school, Ratanlal pursued Electrical Engineering at Malaviya Regional Engineering College (now MNIT) in Jaipur. His intelligence and problem-solving skills soon became legendary. I remember a time when a major fault at a plant near Ganganagar stumped even the experts from BHEL. The executives called upon Ratanlal, whose reputation preceded him, and he resolved the issue, showcasing his exceptional capabilities. Despite his potential to retire as a Chief Engineer, an unfortunate incident of a heart attack led to his early demise.

Jugal Kishore Poddar and Kamlesh Kanak were two other close childhood friends of mine, who are currently in

Jaipur. We all studied together in Poddar school and also met during the evening tuitions at the 'Study Circle.'

Udaipur Life: A Crucible of Challenges and Growth

At that time, the educational system was such structured that after passing the 11th board exams, university education began. The graduation program was typically three years long, but I decided to pursue a degree in agriculture, which was a four-year program. The path to higher education is seldom straightforward, and my journey was no exception.

During my BSc in Agriculture (1964-68) in Udaipur, a city renowned for its majestic palaces and serene lakes, I found myself living in the most unexpected of places, a temple complex *(The Asthal Mandir)*. These years were transformative, imparting not only academic knowledge but also instilling a deeper understanding of perseverance and the value of hard work. My time at Sukhadia University, though extended, was a crucial chapter in my life, laying the groundwork for my future endeavours in agriculture and beyond.

In 1964, when I set off for Udaipur to pursue my graduation in agriculture, I was just 16 years old. My father, who accompanied me, understood the financial constraints we faced and was determined to ensure I received higher education. He left me at the *Asthal Mandir*, which managed accommodation facilities for students who were financially constrained.

This humble beginning marked the start of my life's most challenging yet rewarding journey. It was a place of worship, but for me, it became a sanctuary of learning, resilience, and growth. I stayed in the temple for about one and a half years and later lived in two to three different rented rooms with my friend Mr. Gauri Shankar Paliwal.

My years in Udaipur were characterised by a relentless pursuit of knowledge amidst financial adversity. The city's vibrant culture and historical grandeur were a stark contrast to my humble existence. Yet, it was this contrast that taught me invaluable lessons in endurance and resourcefulness. Udaipur, with its palaces and lakes, was a city of dreams, and amidst its splendour, I nurtured my own dreams.

The journey to graduation was fraught with challenges. I vividly remember the countless nights spent poring over textbooks. These experiences, though harsh, instilled in me a profound sense of gratitude and a deep appreciation for every opportunity that came my way.

When I went to Udaipur for college, it was a mix of highs and lows. While my academic performance was excellent, college life itself was not always smooth. Initially, there was a lot of ragging, which was quite different from what I had experienced earlier. It was obvious to the seniors that I was a new student. They began to pick on me and tried to embarrass me at times. However, I was confident and stood my ground, telling them that their behaviour wouldn't fly with me.

I had moved from Jaipur to attend an agricultural college, where most students came from farming or village backgrounds. This added to the cultural and social challenges I faced. During one ragging session, a senior stepped in and saved me from further harassment. That incident helped me navigate the ragging culture a bit better.

Temple Complex and Early Friendships

My father left me at the temple hostel in Udaipur without much money. This was the point where my struggle for life truly began. It was a harsh initiation into adulthood but one that shaped my character and resilience. Despite the hardships, I faced these challenges with determination. Money was always short, but I managed to navigate these difficulties with remarkable calm.

Life in Udaipur was a daily struggle. I had to cook my meals with whatever resources I could gather. With no cycle or any means of transport, I often walked around 10 kilometres. I was determined not to abandon my education and return home without a degree. The thought of giving up never crossed my mind; instead, each hardship reinforced my commitment to persevere.

In the temple complex hostel, most of the residents were children from nearby villages. We cooked our own meals in our small rooms. Among these students, many went on to become successful IAS and IPS officers. The temple's Mahant Ji (Head Priest) initially helped me a little, but as time went on, I had to rely more on my own resources.

At just 16 years of age, I was the first member of my family to leave home, making every challenge more daunting. However, fortune favoured me, and I met some incredible people who helped me immensely. One of them was Mr. Gauri Shankar Paliwal, a classmate of mine, and his elder brother, Mr. Navneetlal Paliwal. They treated me like their own brother. Whenever I visited their home, they made sure I was treated just like their younger siblings. The Paliwals hailed from a nearby village, where they would sometimes go for a visit. Gauri Shankar's mother would often ask, "Why didn't you bring Trilok along?" Their kindness and hospitality made me realise how lucky I was to have found such supportive friends. Despite the financial hardships and the challenges of living away from home at a young age, I was fortunate to have met people who extended a helping hand.

Money Order of a Significant Value: Rupees Twenty!

One particular incident from those days stands out vividly in my memory, illustrating the resourcefulness and resilience that life often demands. One day, I received a money order from my father. It was twenty rupees, a significant amount back then, though it may seem trivial today. I remember holding those notes in my hand, feeling a mix of gratitude and determination. With this money, I had to ensure that my basic needs were met for the foreseeable future.

I shared my plans with my friend, G.S. Paliwal, who accompanied me to the market. Together, we meticulously strategized how to stretch those twenty rupees as far as possible. The first stop was the grain mill, where I bought five kilos of wheat. After cleaning the grains, I had them ground into flour. This was a crucial purchase, as it meant I could make my own chapatis.

Next, we visited the vegetable market. With careful selection, I bought enough vegetables to last several days. But the most impressive feat was setting up my own little kitchen. I bought a small coal stove (angithi), coal, a rolling board and pin (chakla-belan), a spice box (masaledan), essential spices, a cooking pot (patila), and other necessary utensils. All within those twenty rupees!

Plate 5
Ratan Lal Koli, my childhood friend, with whom I shared a lifelong bond. He was one of the most remarkable persons I have known.

Plate no 6
Gauri Shankar Paliwal: My roommate and best friend, who rendered me great help from my very first day in Udaipur

Back at the hostel, I set up my makeshift kitchen in the small room I shared. In the evenings, I would cook simple meals of roti and sabzi. I laid out a 'dari' (a traditional Indian rug) on the floor to sit and eat. At night, the same rug served as my bed, with a sheet spread over it. In the morning, I would roll up my bedding and store it away, transforming the room back into a living space.

Cooking my own meals was not just about saving money; it became a part of my routine that grounded me. There was something deeply satisfying about preparing food with my own hands, even with the limited resources I had. Those days in Udaipur taught me valuable lessons in frugality, self-sufficiency and the importance of making the best out of what one has.

Reflecting on those times, I realise how much that experience shaped me. It wasn't just about surviving on twenty rupees; it was about learning to thrive within constraints. It was about discovering the strength within to overcome challenges and finding joy in the simplest of things. These are lessons that have stayed with me throughout my life, reminding me of the resilience and ingenuity that reside within each of us.

Life Lessons from Udaipur: Trials and Triumphs

The Wise Words of Mahantji

Living in the temple hostel during my college years in Udaipur brought with it a unique blend of spiritual discipline and academic rigour. Every evening, after the temple activities, I would retreat to my small room to prepare my dinner. At just sixteen years old, I had taken on the responsibility of cooking for myself, a task that was both daunting and liberating.

One evening, as I was busy cooking, Mahantji, the temple head, made his rounds. He entered my room, saw me standing over the stove, and asked, "Trilok Raj, did you come here to cook or to study? What is your future?" His words struck me deeply. At that moment, I didn't have an answer. I was just a young boy trying to manage his daily life while pursuing an education. I remained silent, pondering his question.

As time went by, my academic performance began to speak for itself. I consistently ranked among the top five students in my agriculture program, proving to Mahantji, and to myself that I was indeed focused on my studies and my future. His words, though harsh at the time, instilled in me a sense of purpose and determination. They reminded me to always keep my goals in sight, even while managing the necessities of everyday life.

> *"In the pursuit of knowledge, every setback is a lesson, every achievement a triumph."*

A Painful Lesson in Cooking

Another memorable incident from my Udaipur days involved a painful lesson in kitchen safety. Since I was naive to cooking, I had different experiences. One day, after preparing my meal on the small coal stove (angithi), I tried to dispose of the hot coals by placing them in a metal container and covering it with a plate. Without thinking, I picked up the hot griddle (tawa) with my bare hand to place it on top of the container. Instantly, I felt a searing pain as my thumb and two fingers got burned. The pain was excruciating, and I couldn't use my hand for the simplest of tasks.

There I was, with my fingers throbbing and my meal ready but unable to eat it. Hunger and pain combined to create a moment of utter helplessness. I remember tears streaming down my face as I tried to eat with my left hand, struggling to manage even that simple task. It was a night of pain and frustration, but also a night of resilience.

That incident taught me several valuable lessons. First, it underscored the importance of caution and mindfulness in everything one does. Second, it reminded me of the strength that lies within us, enabling us to endure and overcome even the most painful situations. Finally, it highlighted the stark reality of independence; how managing on one's own can bring both freedom and challenges.

Both these instances from my time in Udaipur are etched in my memory, serving as reminders of the resilience and adaptability that life demands. Mahantji's question was a nudge towards self-awareness and long-term focus, while the painful kitchen mishap was a lesson in caution and perseverance. Together, they shaped my journey, teaching me to balance life's immediate demands with my broader aspirations.

A Lesson in Humility: Encountering MT Deshmukh

I remember one instance, during my college years studying Agriculture, one of our lecturers was MT Deshmukh. He was a peculiar and somewhat funny character, known for his unconventional ways. There was a particular incident involving him that has always stayed with me. For a few months, I used to keep a small tuft of hair, a 'choti', which was quite common in my culture but not very familiar to many.

One day, in the middle of a lecture, Deshmukh Sir decided to make a comment about it. He pointed at my choti in front of the entire class and asked, "What is this? An antenna to capture news?" I was taken aback and didn't know how to respond. The entire class burst into laughter, and I could only stand there, silent and somewhat embarrassed.

Years later, I found myself at the Indian Agricultural Research Institute (IARI) pursuing my Ph.D. Coincidentally, Deshmukh Sir was also there, furthering his studies. One day, there was a class he couldn't attend, so he came to my hostel room to catch up on what he had missed. My father happened to be visiting me at the time, and he was resting in my room.

Deshmukh Sir entered and started talking to me, asking about the class and requesting me to explain the material to him. My father watched the interaction curiously. After Deshmukh Sir left, my father asked, "Who was that?" I explained that he was one of my former lecturers. My father was puzzled, trying to reconcile this respectful interaction with the image he had in his mind. That's when I narrated the story of the choti incident to my father. He was amused and slightly taken aback. It was a moment of realisation for me as well. The same person who once made fun of me in class now needed my help to understand the subject matter.

This encounter taught me a valuable lesson in humility and respect. It made me realise that circumstances change and roles reverse, often in unexpected ways. The experience with Deshmukh Sir reminded me to remain humble and to treat everyone with respect, regardless of their position or the situation. It also emphasised the importance of knowledge and mutual support, even with those who might have once ridiculed us.

In the end, it was a moment of growth for both of us. For Deshmukh Sir, perhaps it was a lesson in empathy and humility. For me, it reinforced the idea that every person we encounter in life has something to teach us, and every situation, no matter how uncomfortable, contributes to our personal and professional development.

So, these experiences, though challenging at the time, have become stories of growth and resilience. They are reminders that every obstacle is an opportunity to learn, and every hardship a step towards greater strength and understanding.

Accomplishing the Udaipur Chapter and Approaching New Dimensions in Delhi

Despite the struggles in Udaipur, I was among the top five students in my class, graduating with flying colours. This accomplishment was not just a personal triumph but also a testament to the power of endurance and the unwavering belief in the transformative power of education.

Upon completing my graduation, I set my sights on higher studies. I enrolled in the MSc and later PhD programs at the Indian Agricultural Research Institute (IARI), one of the premier and prestigious institutions of agricultural research and innovation in the Indian subcontinent, popularly known as PUSA Institute, in Delhi.

Little did I know that my time at PUSA Institute would not only advance my academic career but also introduce me to mentors and colleagues who would play a crucial role in my professional journey later.

As I pen down these memories, I am filled with a profound sense of gratitude. Gratitude for the hardships that taught me resilience, for the people who supported me, and for the opportunities that came my way. My early life, with all its challenges and triumphs, was the crucible in which my character was forged, preparing me for the journey ahead.

"Persistence turns obstacles into opportunities."

- Mathew Thomas

Chapter 3:

Nurtured by a Visionary: Journey with Legendary Dr M.S. Swaminathan

Delhi: A New Beginning

The Indian Agricultural Research Institute (IARI), fondly known as the PUSA Institute, has stood as a beacon of agricultural innovation and excellence in India since 1936. Gaining admission here for further studies was a significant milestone, marking the beginning of a crucial new chapter in my life. This period coincided with a transformation in the status of agricultural research in India and the dawn of the Green Revolution.

I was privileged to be part of this prestigious institute, where I chose plant genetics as my specialisation for my MSc (1968–1970). This choice was driven not only by my passion for the subject but also by the remarkable opportunity to learn under the legendary Dr.M.S. Swaminathan, a genetics specialist and the director-general of the institute.

Plate 7
The Indian Agricultural Research Institute (IARI), New Delhi, (PUSA Institute). My Alma mater, where my MSc and PhD journeys shaped my future. (Image Source: https://www.bharatdirectory.in/indian-agricultural-research-institute/i/225)

Little did I know that in Delhi, under Dr. Swaminathan's tutelage, I would learn the true meaning of innovation and dedication in the field of agriculture. This period would mark the beginning of a new phase, one that would see the culmination of years of hard work and the realisation of dreams nurtured under the most challenging circumstances.

The lessons I learnt during my time in Udaipur stayed with me, reinforcing my belief in the power of education and resilience in overcoming life's challenges. Financial constraints, uncertainty, and homesickness were constant companions there, but they also became catalysts for my inner strength. I learned to prioritise, endure, and find joy in small victories.

Delhi: A Turning Point

Leaving Udaipur behind, I embarked on a new journey to Delhi, a city that promised challenges and opportunities in equal measure. I stayed in Udaipur until 1968, and after completing my graduation, I returned to Jaipur for a short while.

During my holidays in Jaipur, I applied for the Indian Forest Service (IFS) exam, an esteemed service related to agriculture. The dates for the IFS exam and my MSc interview at IARI clashed, presenting me with a significant dilemma. The IFS was a prestigious opportunity, but I had to choose between it and pursuing further studies at a reputed institution known for its research and academics.

Ultimately, I chose to advance my studies in Delhi, a decision that would prove to be one of the most critical turning points in my life. Moving to Delhi, a city I had never been to before, and competing for a place in such a prestigious institute was daunting.

The IARI Interview: A Memorable Experience

In those days, admission to the PUSA Institute involved interviews. Today, a written entrance exam determines the selection, but back then, it was an intensive face-to-face evaluation. I vividly remember the day of my interview at IARI. It was one of the most intriguing experiences of my life. With its esteemed reputation, IARI attracted the best students from various universities.

Around 70 students, each a topper from renowned universities across the country, were vying for a spot in this prestigious program. Only ten of us would be selected, and the competition was fierce. My nerves were frayed with anxiety as I waited for my turn, my mind racing with doubts about my ability to clear the interview.

We were called in groups of five. The interview panel was composed of some of the most distinguished names in the field, including Dr. Swaminathan, who was the chairman, and several heads of divisions. There were also representatives from international foundations like the Rockefeller Foundation.

The selection process was intense, and the odds were daunting. Each group of five candidates faced rigorous questioning. In my batch, there were two female candidates, two Sharmas (including myself), and another candidate.

Fortune smiled upon me. When the final list was announced, I was elated to find my name in second place among the ten selected candidates. Interestingly, out of our batch of five, four were selected, including both female candidates and the two Sharmas. This outcome was both surprising and gratifying, highlighting the impartial and unbiased nature of the selection.

This moment marked a significant milestone in my academic journey, instilling in me a sense of accomplishment and a renewed determination to excel. It was a testament to my hard work and determination.

Starting Days in Delhi and Making Lifelong Connections

The transition to Delhi was not without its challenges. However, I was incredibly fortunate to meet Dr. Avatar Krishna Kaul, who was about ten years older than me. From the first day, he treated me like a younger brother, offering guidance and support that made my adjustment to this new environment much smoother.

When I first arrived in Delhi, the vastness of the city was overwhelming, unlike anything I had experienced before. My life at the Indian Agricultural Research Institute (IARI) was a blend of rigorous academic work and vibrant student life, especially in the hostel.

The Laxmikant-Pyarelal Duo

One of the most memorable aspects of my time at IARI was my friendship with Dr. Sheo Prakash Shukla, who hailed from a village near Raipur, Madhya Pradesh (now Chhattisgarh).

He pursued his MSc and PhD in Agronomy during the same years as mine (1968–1973). Although we were in different subject areas, we were incredibly close. During our MSc, we were roommates; during our PhD, we had adjacent rooms in the hostel, and we even shared our room keys. We explored Karol Bagh and Connaught Place on bicycles and often watched films in theatres, making our time at IARI even more enjoyable.

Our adventures and camaraderie were well-known among our peers. Our bond was so strong that we were known among the hostel students as *"Laxmikant-Pyarelal"*, after the famous music director duo of the time. We spent most of our time in each other's rooms, often disturbing one another. Before completing his PhD, Dr. Shukla went to his village, where his marriage was arranged. I carried his clothes from Delhi to his village when I attended the wedding. After his marriage, while he was still pursuing his PhD at IARI, I would playfully snatch his personal letters from his newlywed wife and read them with him. Such was our friendship. Dr. S.P. Shukla later became an advisor at IFFCO and retired from that prestigious position.

Multidisciplinary Exposure at IARI: Adding Versatility and Confidence to My Personality

There was an incident that stands out vividly in my memory. One day, while Dr. Shukla was away, a student came from Kanpur for the entrance interview for the PhD in Agronomy. He was searching for Dr. Shukla for some guidance. As I was sitting in Dr. Shukla's room, he mistook me for him. Being familiar with agronomy too, I engaged him in conversation, answering several of his questions and discussing various agricultural topics.

For nearly an hour, I thoroughly interviewed him on agronomy and suggested the expected questions in his upcoming interview. Later, when Dr. Shukla returned, the gentleman from Kanpur discovered that I was Trilok from Genetics. He was extremely surprised and appreciated my command and in-depth knowledge of agronomy, which was not my primary subject.

Plate 8
Holding our MSc degrees at IARI: Myself with my dear friend SP Shukla (Batch of 1970)

This incident demonstrated the confidence I had developed there. It highlighted the knowledge I had gained and the ease with which I could discuss complex agricultural concepts. At IARI, seminars were a regular part of our academic life, and we often attended courses from different divisions. This interdisciplinary exposure further enhanced my confidence and broadened my understanding of agricultural research as a whole.

"From classroom lessons to life's classroom, every challenge teaches us more than any textbook."

The Academic Journey: MSc and PhD

My time at IARI was divided into two significant phases: my MSc, which lasted two years (1968–1970), and my PhD, which took another three years, from 1970 to 1973. These years were crucial in shaping my academic and professional future.

During my MSc, I delved deep into Genetics, studying under renowned scientists. The rigorous curriculum and competitive environment pushed me to excel. The diverse and dynamic atmosphere at IARI, coupled with the presence of international scholars and researchers, provided a stimulating environment for learning and growth.

My journey took an enriching turn when Dr. Avtar Krishna Kaul, a Kashmiri scholar, became my guide during my MSc. He was a trusted friend who treated me like a younger brother from the very first day. His guidance was invaluable, offering wisdom beyond academic boundaries.

Plate 9
Myself with Dr MS Swaminathan, the Father of Green Revolution in India and the Director of IARI at the time, on the occasion of my MSc convocation (Batch of 1970)

He used to send Christmas and New Year cards to many people, each one personalised, a habit I imbibed from him and continued for many years in Germany, then Nigeria, and even when we returned to India. He was my mentor for almost ten years and was older than me in both age and wisdom. He was exceptionally experienced and smart. In fact, I was his first student for both MSc and PhD.

Later, when he became my guide for my PhD, he had to leave for West Germany before its completion. The same was the case for Dr. Swaminathan, who was a member of the advisory committee for my PhD, but he had to leave to take charge as Director General of ICAR (Indian Council of Agricultural Research) at Krishi Bhawan in Delhi.

As I laboured over my PhD thesis on "Genetics of Protein Content and Quality of Wheat," Dr. Kaul's support provided a steady anchor. Midway through this period, he embarked on his own academic pursuit in West Germany, in the city of Hannover. Despite the physical distance, his encouragement never wavered. He often spoke of the vibrant academic environment in Hannover, fuelling my aspirations. Upon completing my PhD, Dr. Kaul extended an invitation to join him in West Germany. The prospect of reuniting with my mentor and exploring new academic horizons filled me with excitement.

During my time at IARI, I pursued both my MSc and PhD under the mentorship of some of the most renowned scientists in the field, including Dr. M.S. Swaminathan. His influence and leadership in agricultural research were unparalleled, and working in his lab was an honour. Dr. Swaminathan, who recently received the Bharat Ratna, was a key figure in transforming agricultural research in India. A prominent figure in agricultural science, he was a member of the advisory board for my thesis and research work.

He played a crucial role in elevating the status of agricultural research. At that time, the Director-General of the Indian Council of Agricultural Research (ICAR) held the status of an Additional Secretary, while the heads of other research organisations like the Indian Council of Medical Research (ICMR) and the Council of Scientific and Industrial Research (CSIR) were at the Secretary level.

Dr. Swaminathan fought to ensure that the Director-General of ICAR was given equal status to those heading ICMR and CSIR. This recognition was vital for the agricultural sector, as it underscored the importance of agricultural research and its critical role in ensuring food security for the nation. The transformation in the status of agriculture in India, fuelled by the efforts of visionaries like Dr. Swaminathan, was a turning point. It validated the importance of my chosen field and filled me with a sense of pride and purpose.

"Life's hardships are the raw materials from which we forge our strength and resilience."

The Dawn of the Green Revolution in India

My time at the PUSA Institute was not only academically enriching but also historically significant. This was the dawn of the Green Revolution, a transformative era in post-independent Indian history, spearheaded by Dr. M.S. Swaminathan, who was recently honoured posthumously with the 'Bharat Ratna' in

Plate 10
Receiving PhD degree from Dr MS Swaminathan, the Director General of Indian Council of Agricultural Research (ICAR) Krishi Bhawan, at the time (1973). Later Dr Swaminathan was posthumously honoured with 'Bharat Ratna'.

Plate 11
With my parents in the IARI campus, just after receiving the PhD degree..

Plate 12
With my major guide, Dr AK Kaul, on the occasion of my PhD convocation. Dr Kaul specially came from West Germany to witness the occasion

February 2024. Dr. Swaminathan's leadership left an indelible mark on Indian agriculture.

The institute buzzed with research activities poised to revolutionise agricultural productivity in India. This was not merely an educational experience but a front-row seat to a movement that would change the lives of millions of farmers across the nation. Under the able guidance of Dr. Swaminathan and Dr. Kaul, I embarked on my research journey, focusing on genetics, specifically 'Breeding for Hard Bread Type Wheats' during my MSc and 'High Yielding Varieties (HYV) of Wheat' for my Ph.D.

The Green Revolution primarily targeted staple foods like rice and wheat, aiming to enhance their yield and ensure food security for the burgeoning population. Dr. Swaminathan's expertise in wheat genetics provided me with invaluable insights and mentorship. His vision and dedication were inspiring, and working under his tutelage was a privilege that shaped my academic and professional trajectory.

The research environment at PUSA was dynamic and collaborative. Scholars and scientists from various disciplines converged to share ideas and findings, fostering a culture of innovation and critical thinking. The institute was a melting pot of knowledge, with the brightest minds working tirelessly to find solutions to the agricultural challenges facing our country. This collaborative spirit was instrumental in driving the success of the Green Revolution.

Meeting Dr. Norman Borlaug, a Nobel Laureate, the 'Father of the Green Revolution'

One of the most memorable experiences during my time at PUSA was meeting Dr. Norman Borlaug, the Nobel laureate known as the 'Father of the Green Revolution.' Dr.

Borlaug visited our institute two to three times a year, sharing his insights and experiences. His visits were highly anticipated events, and I was fortunate enough to meet him personally. Dr. Borlaug's humility and dedication to improving global food security left a lasting impression on me.

I vividly remember the day I submitted my thesis. It coincided with a ceremony in the plant genetics department where Dr. Borlaug was being felicitated. Seizing the opportunity, I approached him and requested his autograph on my invitation card. That card remains one of my most cherished possessions, a symbol of a pivotal moment in my life.

My thesis focused on the development and analysis of High Yielding Varieties of wheat, a critical component of the Green Revolution. The research was demanding, requiring meticulous experimentation and data analysis. However, the challenge was exhilarating. I spent countless hours in the lab, driven by the desire to contribute to a cause much larger than myself. The knowledge that our work could directly impact the lives of farmers and enhance food security for the nation was a powerful motivator.

Dr. Swaminathan's guidance was instrumental throughout this process. His ability to distil complex concepts into understandable terms and his unwavering support were crucial in helping me navigate the challenges of my research. He encouraged a holistic approach, urging us to consider the socio-economic implications of our work alongside the scientific aspects. This perspective broadened my understanding and underscored the importance of interdisciplinary collaboration in addressing real-world problems.

THE PRESIDENT AND MEMBERS

of the

Indian Society of Genetics and Plant Breeding

cordially invite you to a reception

in honour of

Dr. Norman E. Borlaug

Noble Laureate

at 4.30 P.M. on Tuesday, September 11, 1973
at the Division of Genetics, I. A. R. I., New Delhi

Dr. Borlaug *has kindly agreed to address the members.*

Norman Borlaug
Sept 11, 1973

R.S.V.P.
Dr. H. K. Jain
Secretary

Plate 13 - Invitation card of a ceremony organized on 11th September 1973, in honour of the Noble laureate and Father of Green Revolution, Dr Norman Borlaug. It was the same day of my PhD thesis submission and I managed to get an autograph by Dr Borlaug.

The culmination of my research was the submission of my thesis, a moment of immense pride and satisfaction. It was a testament to years of hard work, perseverance, and the unwavering support of my mentors and peers. The experience at PUSA Institute was transformative.

An Elementary Course in French

During my academic journey, I encountered a fascinating requirement that added a unique dimension to my Ph.D. pursuit in India: the mandate to attain proficiency in either French, Russian or German language. This prerequisite intertwined with the realms of language and cultural exploration.

Initially drawn to the intricacies of German, I embarked on a path to master its nuances. However, the course's extensive duration and demanding schedule posed significant challenges. Balancing rigorous academic commitments alongside language learning became a formidable task, prompting me to reassess my linguistic journey. Adapting to circumstances, I made a strategic shift towards French, a decision influenced by practical considerations and a keen sense of adaptability. Engaging in an elementary course, I navigated through the intricacies of French grammar and vocabulary, earning a certificate that symbolised my newfound proficiency.

Beyond the academic sphere, my linguistic endeavours permeated into personal interactions, notably enriching conversations later with my grandsons, Prabhav, Arjun, and Raghav, who opted for French as a third language in their school. Delving into discussions in French was quite interesting, and I could see the surprise and excitement on their faces.

L'INSTITUT INDIEN DE RECHERCHE AGRONOMIQUE

(ÉCOLE SUPÉRIEURE)

Certifie que ___Mr. T.R. SHARMA_____

a suivi un cours élémentaire de français avec deux cours par semaine de _1 Octobre 1971_ à _30 Sept. 1972_ et a subi avec succès l'examen de passage qui a eu lieu le _23 Octobre 1972_.

_____
Professeur
chargé de cours

_____
Doyen de l'École Supérieure

Nouvelle-Delhi-12, le _16 NOV 1973_ 197

INDIAN AGRICULTURAL RESEARCH INSTITUTE

(POST-GRADUATE SCHOOL)

This is to certify that ___Mr. T.R. SHARMA_____

has attended a French Language Elementary Course of two classes per week from _1 October 1971_ to _30 Sept. 1972_ and has passed the Final Examination held on _23 October 1972_.

_____
Course Teacher

_____
Dean, Post-Graduate School

New Delhi-12, the _16 NOV 1973_ 197

Plate 14
The Certificate of French Language Elementary Course attended at IARI over a duration of one year (Oct,1971 to Sept,1972). My first experience with a foreign language.

A Helping Hand During My MSc Days

When I was completing my MSc at IARI, I found myself in a bit of a financial bind. I needed funds to complete my thesis writing, so I decided to reach out to an old friend, Gauri Shankar Paliwal, for help. I wrote him a letter, requesting him to send me 200 rupees. To my surprise, within a few days, I received a telegraphic money order for 190 rupees. In his letter, he explained that he was about to go on a tour and would be away for 8-10 days. Just before leaving, he received my letter. He had exactly 200 rupees at home, so he sent me 190 rupees after deducting the small fee required for the money order.

This act of friendship left a deep impression on me. Even today, our bond remains strong. When his grandson got married, I was personally invited to the wedding. The simple act of sending 190 rupees back then not only helped me during a crucial time but also solidified a lifelong friendship.

Chapter 4

An Energetic Soul Captivated by Movies, Music, and Literature

Passion for Cinema and Music

As a child, my father was strictly against watching movies, so I rarely saw any, except a couple of them with my close friend Mr. Ratan Lal Koli. Later, in 1964, when I went to Udaipur for further studies, I stayed in a hostel at a temple (The Asthal Mandir), where the Mahant Ji, the head priest, was also against students watching films. However, in 1966, while living with my friend Mr. G.S. Paliwal in a rented room, I began to develop an interest in watching movies.

We also had a common friend, and every Wednesday, we would gather to listen to the famous *Binaca Geet Mala* on the radio, hosted by Mr. Ameen Sayani. Listening to his engaging presentation of songs was a delightful experience. This was the first radio countdown show of Indian film songs, which was initially broadcast on Radio Ceylon and later on the Vividh Bharti service of All India Radio. It had millions of listeners and is considered the most popular show in the history of radio programs, starting in 1953.

The most memorable episode was the 1000th, aired on October 25, 1972, featuring the top and most popular song of each year since the show's beginning in 1953. I was so fascinated by this show that I still have the list of these songs, in my handwriting, preserved for the last 52 years. Alongside the songs, I noted other related details, including the films, producers, lyricists, singers, music directors, and major actors. I even created a list of 'films to be seen' based on this historic episode.

When I visited Jaipur, I would watch films and, upon returning to Udaipur, watch the same movies again because they would be released there a bit later. This led me to see many films more than once. In 1968, when I went to Bombay to represent the Faculty of Agriculture at the All India Teachers and Students camp, I watched five to six films during a week's stay, including one or two at the famous Maratha Mandir theatre. My teacher, Dr. A.K. Kaul, in Germany, was amazed by my knowledge of films.

It's challenging to pick just one or two favourite films, but *Mother India* and *Sholay* have always been my top choices. *Mother India* closely depicts the life of rural India, particularly the farming community in the 1940s and 1950s. Such situations still exist to some extent. It became India's first submission for the Academy Award for Best Foreign Language Film in 1958. The film beautifully portrays the plight of farmers at the hands of moneylenders. On the other hand, *Sholay* is very entertaining, with a lot of action, and Amjad Khan's role as Gabbar Singh has become iconic.

Language or country never became a barrier in my passion for cinema. Even in Germany, I continued to watch movies. In the English category, my favourite film is *The Sound of Music*, released in 1965. The movie is entertaining, and the songs are melodious, with "Doe a Deer" being particularly famous. I liked this movie because I saw it in Germany, and I visited the places where it was shot in Salzburg and its beautiful, green surroundings. The film is based on a true story about a family that fled Austria to the USA, terrified by the Nazi atrocities as they invaded Austria.

In Germany, I also had the opportunity to see classic movies in a theatre run by the British Army. An acquaintance from the army helped us with passes, as these films were specially screened for military personnel. Some memorable ones include the uncensored version of *The Exorcist* (1973), *Jaws* (1975), *The Godfather* (1972), *Earthquake* (1974), *The Towering Inferno* (1974), and *Dial M for Murder* (1954), among others!

Interest in Books and Literature

I am a slow reader by nature, and these days I don't read much except for some Vipassana literature. However, during my time in Germany (1974-1977), Nigeria (1978-1988), and India (1988-1995), I read a lot of Indian and English literary works, both fiction and non-fiction.

In Germany and Nigeria, we were regular readers of the weekly *Time* magazine and *Newsweek*. In India, we subscribed to *Reader's Digest* and *Science Reporter* for a few years, which our children also enjoyed.

Among the books I cherish most is *The Story of My Experiments with Truth*, the autobiography of Mahatma Gandhi. The book covers his early childhood, law education, and journey of becoming a barrister in London. It also details his life in South Africa, where he faced discrimination and began his 'Satyagraha' movement, which means holding fast to truth. Gandhi's stay in South Africa for nearly 21 years (1893-1914) is beautifully described, along with his struggles and contributions to India's freedom movement, which culminated in independence in 1947.

As for English fiction, one book that stands out is *The Day of the Jackal* by Frederick Forsyth. The novel, a thrilling blend of fiction and non-fiction, is hard to put down once you start. A movie adaptation has also been made.

During my Ph.D. in India, I improved my English by reading the *Screen* magazine, a popular weekly film publication. This was not only for enhancing my English but also due to my keen interest in movies, especially Hindi films. I was so captivated by the magazine that despite its bulkiness, I would read almost all the pages within the week, eagerly awaiting the next issue.

In retrospect, I realise how my passion for cinema and literature broadened my understanding of various aspects of life, shaping me into a more accomplished, multifaceted, and versatile individual. Music served as a companion during times when I had to live alone, away from my family.

Recognizing my love for music, a few years ago, on my birthday, my daughters gifted me a *Saregama Carvaan*, a digital audio player with 5,000 preloaded evergreen songs of different genres. With evolving interests over the years, I now occasionally use it to play spiritual content like *Vipassana Dohe* (couplets).

The Legacy Carried Forward

It's heartening to see that my son, Ankur, had also developed an interest in books and literature. We still proudly maintain his wonderful collection, which includes philosophy, intriguing fiction, notable biographies and autobiographies, and other renowned literature.

I'm delighted to see my grandsons (Sangita's sons), Prabhav (Ricky) and Arjun, carrying forward the passion for reading and literature.

It gives me immense happiness to see their collection at such a young age, including *Atomic Habits*, *The Power of Your Subconscious Mind*, *Wings of Fire* (an autobiography of Dr. APJ Abdul Kalam), stories by Ruskin Bond, Sherlock Holmes, Sudha Murty, the entire Harry Potter series, and the epics of *Ramayana* and *Mahabharata*, apart from the Science Encyclopedia.

This virtue is likely passed down from their father too, my elder son-in-law, Dr. Vaibhav, who has a great interest in Hindi literature and philosophy.

Chapter 5

Green Revolution to World Class Research: Post Doctoral Pursuits in Germany

Journey to Germany: A Transformative Chapter

After completing my PhD, a new chapter in my life unfolded when Dr. A.K. Kaul, my esteemed guide and friend, invited me to join him in Germany for postdoctoral research. At that time, Germany was still divided into East and West, and the offer was a prestigious opportunity that I couldn't refuse. It promised to take me to the Technical University of Hannover in West Germany, a place known for its excellence in research and innovation.

From 1974 to 1977, my time in Germany was transformative, both professionally and personally. Reflecting on my decision to pursue further studies at the Indian Agricultural Research Institute (IARI) over the Indian Forest Service (IFS) exam, I realise it was pivotal.

Plate 15
Rajasthan Patrika (one of the leading newspapers in India), 18th November, 1974: News on my invitation from The Technical University of Hannover (West Germany) and my departure from India. Going abroad was not so common in those days and thus brought happiness and pride to my parents and family.

Plate 15a
With Dr AK Kaul and his family in Hannover, West Germany

The experiences and opportunities I encountered in Delhi were invaluable, not only for my academic growth but also for my personal development and resilience. Delhi became a turning point, setting the stage for a career that would eventually take me to international heights and cement my place in the field of agricultural research.

The Initial Challenge: Obtaining a Passport

Securing a passport in the 1970s was no small feat. It required a trip to Delhi, navigating bureaucratic red tape, and waiting with bated breath for the precious document that would open doors to international horizons. The process posed a significant challenge as I needed signatures from various officials. This often involved under-the-table dealings, adding complexity to the already daunting task.

I vividly remember visiting multiple offices, from collectors to judicial magistrates, seeking signatures and approvals. It seemed nearly impossible to get the necessary signatures on the passport application form. Faced with these hurdles, I considered travelling to Delhi for the process, hoping to leverage my connections. I knew influential people like Dr. Swaminathan, who held a secretary-level position and was the Director General of the Indian Council of Agricultural Research (ICAR). Additionally, through my father, I was acquainted with few individuals in Delhi, including the Private Secretary to the Cabinet Secretary working in the President House (who later became my father-in-law). I was confident their assistance could expedite the process.

Despite the cumbersome process, I eventually managed to secure the signature of a deputy secretary in Jaipur, who sympathised with my situation. With that signature, my passport application was finally processed.

Holding the passport in my hands symbolised more than just the permission to travel; it marked the beginning of an exciting new journey. The prospect of travelling overseas was both thrilling and daunting. Overseas travel was not common at that time, and it was a momentous occasion for my family. They were delighted yet apprehensive about my venturing into unknown territories, away from familiar surroundings.

The challenges I faced in obtaining my passport were just the beginning of a journey that would shape my career and life in profound ways. Little did I know then that this journey would lead to international recognition and open doors to new opportunities and experiences.

My Role at the Technical University of Hannover:

Embarking on my post-doctoral journey in Germany, I joined the Institut für Strahlen Botanik (Institute for Radiation Botany) in the Technical University of Hannover as a Postdoctoral Research Fellow. From 1974 to 1976, I spent the first year and a half immersing myself in the intensive research environment. The faculty and students were incredibly disciplined and focused, reflecting the meticulous nature for which Germans are renowned.

Although English was not widely spoken, I found that many people understood it and could converse to some extent. This was a relief, as it eased my transition into this new cultural and academic landscape.

Halfway through my fellowship, in 1976, I received a faculty position as a research scientist at the Institut für Biophysik (Institute for Biophysics), another institute in the Technical University of Hannover. This was a significant milestone, both professionally and personally. It validated the hard work and dedication I had put into my studies and research. As a faculty member, my responsibilities centred on research rather than teaching, allowing me to delve deeper into my work. This role enabled me to impart knowledge and mentor the next generation of researchers, adding depth to my professional journey. At the Technical University of Hannover, I had the privilege of interacting with some of the brightest minds in agricultural research. My colleagues were welcoming and collaborative.

Germany, with its rich history and vibrant culture, was a stark contrast to the world I had known in India. The institutes here were smaller than the sprawling campuses back home, yet they were equipped with world-class research facilities. This was a place where innovation thrived. I immersed myself in research, eager to absorb as much knowledge and experience as possible. The state-of-the-art facilities and academic rigour pushed me to new heights.

I continued my work in quality assurance, focusing on improving food quality standards. My expertise in this area led to collaborations with renowned institutions and researchers, further solidifying my reputation in the field.

"International collaborations broaden horizons and deepen understanding."

Plate 16
Institut für Biophysik (Institute for Biophysics) at the Technical University of Hannover, where I worked as a Research Scientist in a Faculty Position.

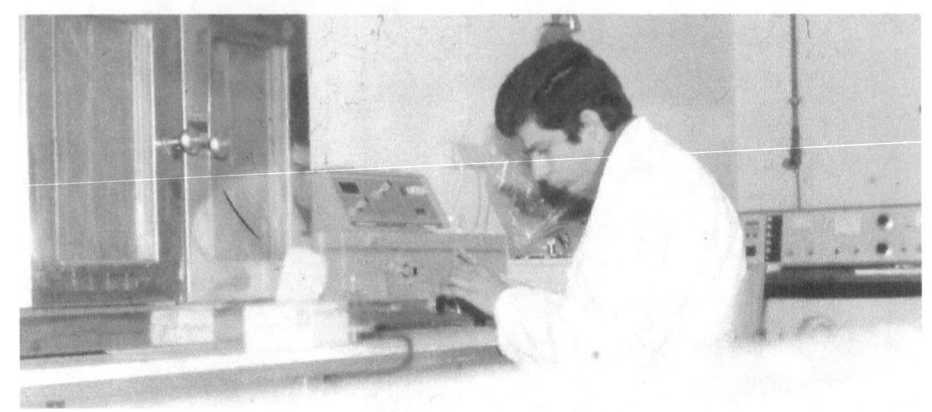

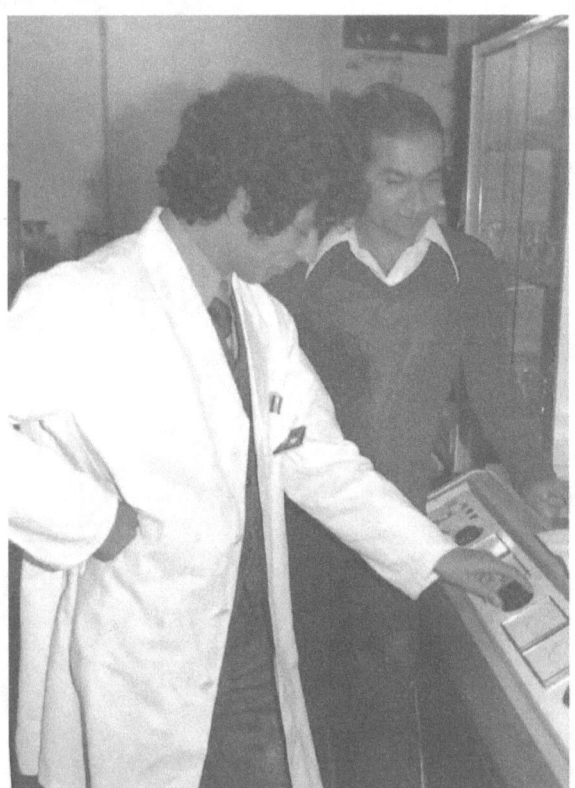

Plate 17a & 17b
Immersed in Research Work at the Technical University of Hannover, West Germany, 1975

International Recognition and Achievements

My contributions to the field of food quality did not go unnoticed. I received international recognition for my work, including invitations to speak at conferences and seminars. These opportunities showcased my expertise and broadened my horizons, exposing me to diverse perspectives and honing my skills as a researcher and educator. The experiences and lessons I learned during this period laid the groundwork for my future endeavours. The postdoctoral research I conducted during these years laid the foundation for my future contributions to agricultural science.

Working on advanced projects and collaborating with esteemed researchers expanded my knowledge and expertise. It was a time of intense intellectual growth, pushing the boundaries of what I thought possible. The research we conducted and our findings were published in prestigious British, American, and German journals. Seeing our work recognized on such esteemed platforms was incredibly rewarding. I still keep the hard copies of those publications in a file with me.

Germany taught me the value of resilience and adaptability. It showed me that no matter where life takes us, maintaining our core values and embracing new cultures can lead to growth and success. The bonds I formed, the knowledge I gained, and the experiences I lived through continue to influence my journey. The German chapter is a part of my life that I hold close to my heart.

Reprinted from **AGRICULTURAL AND FOOD CHEMISTRY**, Vol. 25, No. 1, Page 200, Jan./Feb. 1977
Copyright 1977 by the American Chemical Society and reprinted by permission of the copyright owner.

Nutritive Value of Rye and Wheat Breads Assessed with *Aspergillus flavus*

The relative nutritive value of crust and crumb portions of rye and wheat breads has been assessed using the fungus *Aspergillus flavus*. Rye bread crumb was rated superior to wheat bread crumb. Crusts of both the breads showed a reduced nutritive value. The fungus graded these samples in the same order as has been done by the protozoan *Tetrahymena pyriformis* and by rat bioassays using the same material.

Plate 18
My research on Rye and Wheat Breads published in the American Journal of Agricultural and Food Chemistry, 1977

Evaluation of Relative Nutritive Value in Cultivars of Triticale with Shrivelled Grain Characteristics, Using *Aspergillus flavus*

Mirza Mohyuddin, Trilok R. Sharma and Ernst G. Niemann

Institut für Strahlenbotanik, Herrenhäuser Str. 2, 3000 Hannover, Federal Republic of Germany

(Manuscript received 22 July 1977)

Z. Anal. Chem. 280, 133–138 (1976) — © by Springer-Verlag 1976

Rapid Determination of Nitrogen Content in Grain-Meal Samples with Alkali-Phenol Reaction, Manually and with an Autoanalyzer

A. K. Kaul* and T. R. Sharma

Institut für Strahlenbotanik der GSF, Hannover

Received October 1, 1975

Use of *Aspergillus flavus* to Evaluate the Relative Nutritive Value in Cultivars of Rye, Wheat and Triticale

Mirza Mohyuddin, Trilok R. Sharma, Avtar K. Kaul[a] and Ernst G. Niemann

Institut für Strahlenbotanik, Herrenhäuser Str. 2, 3000 Hannover, Federal Republic Germany

(Manuscript received 15 April 1976)

Mirza Mohyuddin*
Trilok Raj Sharma
Ernst-Georg Niemann

Institut für Strahlenbotanik
Gesellschaft fur Strahlen-und Umweltforschung
3000 Hannover, West Germany

Received for review May 24, 1976. Accepted October 4, 1976. One of us (M.M.) acknowledges the financial assistance of Alexander von Humboldt Foundation, Bonn, West Germany.

Plate 18a
Our Research Work and findings published in prestigious German, British and American Journals.

STUDY OF THE INHERITANCE OF GRAIN WEIGHT AND PROTEIN CONTENT IN WHEAT (TRITICUM AESTIVUM L.) BASED ON SINGLE GRAIN ANALYSIS

T. R. SHARMA[1], S. K. BANERJEE and A. K. KAUL[1]

Indian Agricultural Research Institute,
New Delhi, India

Z. Pflanzenzüchtg. 76, 204—214 (1976)
© 1976 Verlag Paul Parey, Berlin und Hamburg
ISSN 0044-3208 / ASTM-Coden: ZEPZAD

*From Institut für Strahlenbotanik,
Gesellschaft für Strahlen- und Umweltforschung mbH., Hannover*

Rationale of Using Dye-Binding Capacity (DBC) for the Evaluation of Protein Content and Quality in Segregating Lines of Wheat

By

T. R. SHARMA and A. K. KAUL

With 6 figures and 2 tables

Received September 23, 1975

Plate 18b
Our Research Work and findings published in prestigious German, British and American Journals.

Lessons from Germany: Embracing Discipline in Life

One of the positive aspects of life in Germany was the emphasis on discipline. For instance, if the traffic lights turned red at midnight, pedestrians would wait patiently until the signal turned green, even if there were no cars in sight. This disciplined approach extended to all aspects of life, creating a sense of order and efficiency. The strict adherence to rules and regulations was evident not just on the roads but also in everyday activities. People would follow designated paths and lanes, even if it meant walking a bit longer. This discipline ensured smooth operations and minimised chaos, making life more organised and predictable.

This level of discipline was particularly striking and contrasted sharply with the more relaxed attitudes I later encountered in Paris, London, and Amsterdam. In Germany, the disciplined approach was ingrained in the culture, fostering a sense of responsibility and respect for regulations. This disciplined lifestyle had a profound impact on my outlook and behaviour. It taught me the value of respecting rules and routines, leading to greater efficiency and productivity in my personal and professional life. The German experience instilled in me a sense of discipline that I carry with me to this day, shaping my approach to challenges and opportunities.

My initial days in Germany were filled with a mix of awe and adaptation. The university environment was rigorous and demanding, yet it fostered a culture of excellence and innovation. One of the most memorable aspects of my time in Germany was my growing reputation for punctuality and discipline. These traits, ingrained in me from my upbringing and honed through years of dedication, stood out even among the Germans.

During my time in Germany, I had the opportunity to travel to various parts of Europe. Each city, each country, had its unique charm and cultural nuances. Paris dazzled with its romance and artistry, London impressed with its blend of tradition and modernity, and Amsterdam fascinated with its canals and liberal spirit. These travels enriched my life, offering insights into different ways of living and thinking. Yet, it was Germany that left the most profound impact on me. The country's emphasis on discipline, efficiency, and innovation resonated deeply with my values.

Settling into German Life

The transition from the bustling streets of India to the serene landscapes of Germany was not just a change of place but a metamorphosis of the soul. It was a journey that unfolded like a symphony, each note resonating with emotions of excitement, curiosity, and a touch of apprehension.

When I embarked on my journey to Germany, I never imagined how profoundly it would shape my understanding of the world and my place within it. What I didn't expect were the deep connections I would form and the cultural lessons I would learn, which would stay with me forever.

One of the first families I became close to in Germany was the Topka family. Their warmth and hospitality were a welcome reprieve from the challenges of adjusting to a new country. Marianne and Wolfgang, the Topkas' daughter and her partner, were living together before marriage, a norm in the West that initially surprised me. In India, such an arrangement would be frowned upon, but in Germany, it was a common and accepted practice. Marianne and Wolfgang later got married, and their relationship became a beautiful example of love and companionship.

Being surrounded by peers in my age group was comforting, and we often spent time together exploring the city, sharing meals, and engaging in deep conversations about life, friendships, and career aspirations. I also formed another group with students from the institute, which allowed me to stay intellectually stimulated and socially active.

As I adapted to the German way of life, the most striking change was the shift in transportation culture. In India, the scooter was our faithful companion, weaving through chaotic traffic with familiarity. Owning a car was a distant dream, and swimming seemed like an exotic skill reserved for the privileged few. However, Germany introduced me to a new lifestyle, where cars were not just a luxury but a commonality, and swimming was a life skill embraced by all. Swimming and driving were both very popular there.

In Hannover, there was an Olympic-sized swimming pool that we visited every few weeks. Swimming was such a common activity that my initial inability to swim made me feel like an outsider among my German friends. I remember sticking to the part of the pool marked for kids, feeling somewhat embarrassed but determined to learn. Over time, I picked up the basics of swimming, an achievement that boosted my confidence and helped me integrate further into the local culture.

Plate 19
Myself with our German friends, Marianne and Wolfgang at their residence.

Plate 20
With Mr and Mrs Topka (Marianne's Parents)

Plate 21
Enjoying the winter chill at the Frozen Maschee Lake with an Indian friend, Hannover, 1975
(Myself standing on the left)

It was common for my German friends to drive, and having a car provided a sense of freedom and mobility to them, which fascinated me. Later, during another chapter of my life in Nigeria in 1978, we bought a Volkswagen Beetle and enjoyed rides with it for the next 10 years.

Language Adventures in Germany

My time in Germany was not just about research and academia; it was also a journey of language exploration and cultural immersion. One of the most fascinating challenges I faced was learning the language. German is known for its systematic and complex grammar, and mastering it was no easy feat.

In addition to research, I enrolled in a German language course at an institute offering evening classes. For around eleven months, I dedicated myself to studying German grammar from *Carl Duisberg Gesellschaft (CDG)*. The intricacies of the language intrigued me, and I soon found myself not only speaking it to some extent but also excelling in its grammatical aspects.

These classes were lively and interactive, with a mix of Indo-German friends and engaging activities. Our teacher, in his mid-60s, had a jovial nature and a remarkable sense of humour. He often joked about shaking hands with Hitler in his youth, adding a humorous touch to our language learning sessions.

I still remember a hilarious yet enlightening incident that highlighted the intricacies of language and cultural understanding. We had a young couple join our group; the lady was fluent in English and knew some French but was not familiar with German. One day, during a casual conversation, someone asked her in English, "What do you do in the night?" The lady, not understanding the question properly, replied with a smile. Her face turned slightly red as she realised the misunderstanding caused by the question's phrasing. In German, the question could mean something entirely different!

After a moment of laughter and explanation, it was clarified that the question was about evening activities, not anything inappropriate. This incident showcased the importance of language nuances and the need for clear communication, especially in multilingual settings.

One memorable experience was when I met the Topka family, whose daughter, Marianne, was studying at the university. During a conversation, Marianne made a grammatical error in German, which I promptly corrected, earning appreciation from her mother, Mrs. Lilo Topka. This further boosted my confidence in speaking German. Through these experiences, I not only improved my language skills but also gained a deeper understanding of cultural nuances and the importance of clear communication in cross-cultural interactions.

Learning the Egalitarian Approach: Respect for All

Germans had a unique approach to vacations, or "Urlaub." Unlike in many other countries, vacations in Germany were seen as an essential part of life. People took their time off seriously, using it to recharge and explore new places. It wasn't just about the break itself but also about the respectful way vacations were treated in professional settings.

I recall an instance when the director of our institute greeted a returning technician by asking about his holiday. Such interactions were rare in India, where hierarchical boundaries often prevented such casual, respectful exchanges between different levels of staff.

This ethos of treating everyone with respect, regardless of their position, left a deep impression on me. Years later, when I was about to retire in Bikaner, India, I wished a peon a happy birthday by shaking hands with him. The news spread through the office, and while some colleagues advised against such familiarity with subordinates, I stood by my actions. The inclusive work ethic I had learned in Germany had become a core part of my values, reinforcing my belief that every worker deserves to be treated with dignity and respect.

Reflecting on this incident, I realised the valuable lessons I had imbibed from my experiences during my stay in Germany. The importance of humility, the neutrality of time, and the avoidance of hierarchical distinctions were key principles I had imbibed.

Retrospectively, I realise how crucial they were in shaping my outlook on life and work. The discipline, respect for rules, and the egalitarian approach I observed in Germany were vastly different from what I had known in India. These experiences broadened my perspective and enriched me, both personally and professionally.

Chapter 6

Homecoming and the Harmonious Arranged Union

Returning to India in April 1977 felt like stepping into a different world. The country was under the state of 'Emergency' imposed by Indira Gandhi's government, and the political climate was charged with tension.

After spending two and a half enriching years in Germany, I found the transition both challenging and invigorating. My return to India was marked not only by a family reunion but also by a significant personal milestone, my marriage. This chapter of my life began with a letter from my future father-in-law, Shri Ram Swaroop Ji Sharma, who was the Under Secretary (General Administration) and Private Secretary to the Cabinet Secretary of India (President House, New Delhi).

It was a proposal for an arranged marriage, a common practice in India. Despite my initial hesitation, I trusted my parents to make the right decision for me. After all, they had been my guiding lights throughout my life.

Plate 22
My proposal photograph, a usual practice at the time, taken in Jaipur, 1977

Plate 23
Miss Krishna's proposal photograph, clicked in 1976 in New Delhi. Later we got married in June, 1977

The letter arrived while I was still in Germany. I responded cautiously, stating that the decision would ultimately rest with my parents. When I finally landed in Delhi, my parents were there to greet me with open arms. Their conviction that this marriage proposal was the right match for me was palpable. My father, a respected member of our community with numerous connections, and my mother assured me that this was a good match. Their confidence was all I needed to agree.

Our meeting with my future in-laws was memorable. They were educated, humble, and welcoming individuals who immediately made me feel at home. My wife-to-be, a poised and intelligent woman, had completed a diploma in Business Administration and was working at Engineering Projects India Limited (EPI). She had also completed her BSc, BEd, and MEd. Our initial conversations were brief, but they were enough for me to realise that she was someone I could build a life with. The proposal was finalised the very next day, and our families began preparing for the wedding.

Financial stability was one of the many gifts my time in Germany had bestowed upon me. As a faculty member, I had earned a good amount of money, which allowed me to ensure a comfortable start to our married life. I brought back enough savings to make the necessary arrangements for my wife. Unlike many traditional marriages in India, our union was not based on the exchange of dowry, a practice I was firmly against. My principles and the support of my family ensured that our marriage was founded on mutual respect and love, not material transactions.

R.S.Sharma.
P.S. to Cabinet Secretary.

(157)

Cabinet Secretariat,
Rashtrapati Bhavan,
New Delhi,
17.11.1976.

Dear Dr. Tirlok Raj,

    Last week I had the privilege of meeting your father who had come to Delhi. During the course of our talk it transpired that you were likely to come to India either in December 76 or in April/May 77, and your marriage is also to be performed at that time. I subsequently sent word to your father enquiring whether the proposal regarding my daughter would be acceptable to him. Subject to your final concurrence, he would be agreeable and therefore I am writing this letter to find out your final views. May be that your father may also write to you in this regard. As you are aware my daughter is B.Sc., M.Ed., Dip. in Business Administration, 25 yrs. 5 ft tall, slim, fair, employed getting Rs 1150/- p.m. Our family details are known to you all and there is no need for me to recapitulate them again.

    Why I have taken the liberty of writing to you direct is the instance of your father so that we know in clear terms whether the proposal is acceptable to you all or not. I had not pursued this matter earlier because someone gave me to understand that your marriage has been settled. I am glad I met your father and got the clarification. Hence this letter. As I am keen to finalise this issue at an (early date) I would very much appreciate your (reply) early. Please also let me know the firm date of your arrival in India.

    With all good wishes, I hope you are doing well there.

Yours sincerely,
(R.S.Sharma)

Plate 24
Marriage Proposal I received from my future father in law, Shri Ram Swaroopji Sharma, the Under Secretary (General Administration) and the Private Secretary to the Cabinet Secretary, Cabinet Secretariat, Rashtrapat Bhavan, New Delhi. I received this letter in Hannover, West Germany.

From,
T.R. Sharma,
Institut für Biophysik,
Herrenhäuserstr.2,
3000 Hannover,
<u>FRG</u>

22nd December 1976

To,
Shri R.S. Sharma,
Private Secretary to
Cabinet Secretary,
Cabinet Secretariat,
Rashtrapati Bhawan,
New Delhi 110004,
<u>INDIEN</u>

    Respected Sharmaji,

    Thanks for your letter dated 17th Dec. 1976. I am sorry that I could not reply you soon. In the meantime, however, I have also heard from my parents. I can very well imagine that you would be very keen to finalise the marriage of your daughter. However, I find it really very hard to make any commitment just by sitting here, as the final decision would be reached with the consent of all the members of my family. How can I, therefore, write 'yes' or 'no' straight forward. I sincerely hope that you would appreciate my situation.

    I have not yet finalised the programme, when I would be coming to India. But, I believe that it would be somewhere in the first week of April next year. My work is going on well here.

    With best personal regards and wishing you and everyone in the family a happy and prosperous New Year, I remain

    Sincerely yours,

    [signature]

    (Trilok Raj Sharma)

Plate 25
My reply to the marriage proposal. A letter from Institut fur Biophysik, Hannover to the Cabinet Secretariat, Rashtrapati Bhavan, New Delhi.

The days leading up to the wedding were a whirlwind of emotions. There was a sense of anticipation, tinged with the bittersweet realisation that life was about to change in profound ways. Yet, amidst the flurry of preparations, there was an underlying feeling of contentment, a knowingness that this union was meant to be.

Finally, on 1st June, 1977, our wedding day arrived, marking the culmination of our journey from strangers to life partners. The wedding procession travelled from Jaipur to IIT Delhi, near which my father-in-law's house stands to this day. His esteemed position in the government added a sense of gravitas to the occasion, making it a memorable affair filled with blessings and well-wishes.

"Marriage is the intertwining of destinies, where two paths converge to create a new journey together."

It was a joyous affair, attended by family and friends. Marianne and her mother, Mrs. Lilo Topka, travelled all the way from Germany to attend our wedding. Among the distinguished guests was Mr. Nirmal Kumar Mukarji, the last ICS officer (Indian Civil Service) of India (ICS 1943) and the Cabinet Secretary of the Government of India at that time.

My father-in-law was associated with him as the Private Secretary to the Cabinet Secretary. We, the newlywed couple, were fortunate to have Mr. Mukarji bless our marriage. We had a brief discussion during which he inquired about life in West Germany, possibly due to his previous visits there. The celebration was filled with laughter, blessings, and the promise of a new beginning.

Plate 26
The day of our marriage, 1st June, 1977, New Delhi. Exchanging Garlands; 'The Varmala'

Plate 27
The 'Phere': myself and my wife, Krishna, being blessed by my Father in law, Shri Ram Swaroopji Sharma (standing on the left side) and my Father, Shri Mangilalji Sharma (standing on the right side).

My father-in-law and mother-in-law's humility and warmth made the transition smooth for both of us. They treated me like their own son and extended the same affection to my family. After the wedding, we faced the logistical challenge of securing a passport for my wife. Remarkably, her passport was ready in just thirteen days, along with our marriage registration certificate, visa, and air tickets; a feat quite uncommon in those days. This was a testament to the efficient and humble nature of my father-in-law, who held a senior position yet remained grounded and approachable.

By 13th June, 1977, we were on our way back to Germany, ready to embark on this new chapter together. My wife adapted quickly to the new environment, and we began to build our life together. She supported me in my work and embraced the challenges of living in a foreign country with grace. Our life in Germany was a blend of professional dedication and personal growth. We explored the rich cultural landscape, from historical sites to vibrant local festivals.

As I navigated the nuances of married life, I realised that the true essence of marriage lies not in grand gestures or dramatic changes but in the everyday moments of togetherness and companionship. It's about finding harmony amidst the chaos, celebrating the differences, and growing together through life's myriad experiences.

Marriage, for me, was not just a union of two individuals but a fusion of dreams, aspirations, and shared responsibilities. It brought a sense of completeness and purpose, shaping me into a better version of myself as I embraced the joys and challenges of this new phase of life.

As I pen down these memories, I am filled with gratitude for the journey that led me to this beautiful chapter of my life; a chapter enriched with love, understanding, and the magic of unforeseen bonds.

Plate 28
The newly wed couple: Mrs Krishna Kumari Sharma and Dr Trilok Raj Sharma (1st June, 1977, New Delhi).

Chapter 7

Together in Deutschland: Journey Back to Germany with Better Half

After our wedding in June 1977, we embarked on a new journey together, returning to Germany as a married couple. This period marked a significant transition in our lives.

Before our marriage, I had lived in a modest single room. Anticipating the need for more space and comfort as a family, I arranged for a fully furnished house before coming to India for the wedding. This new home in Schützenallee, near Maschsee Lake in Hannover, symbolised our fresh start and provided the space where we would build our life together.

Germany was vastly different from India, but it had become a second home to me over the past two and a half years. I was eager to share this experience with my wife. Upon returning to Hannover, we settled into our warm and inviting new home, a perfect setting for the next chapter of our lives. We quickly adapted to our new routine, blending the rich cultural heritage of India with the precision and punctuality of German life.

Plate 29
With the Director of our Institutes, Prof.(Dr) E.G. Niemann and his family on the occasion of the post marriage party for my German colleagues. June, 1977, Hannover, West Germany.

Plate 30a & 30b
Celebrating the Indian Independence day, 15th August, with the Indian Community at Hannover (1977)

One of our first steps was to connect with the Indian community in Germany. Celebrating Indian festivals like Diwali helped us maintain a strong connection to our roots while living abroad. These celebrations were a delightful fusion of traditions, allowing us to share our culture with our German friends and create beautiful memories of cross-cultural exchange.

At my institute, I hosted a wedding party for about 40 people, including colleagues and friends. It was a successful affair, complete with traditional Indian and German cuisine and drinks, which were well-received by our guests. In Germany, it is customary for visitors to bring gifts, such as flowers or drinks, which the host greatly appreciates. Our guests showered us with flowers and warm wishes, making us feel truly blessed and welcomed. Our social circle in Germany expanded as we integrated into the local community. We made friends with neighbours and colleagues, sharing meals and experiences that enriched our understanding of each other's cultures.

Life in Germany was smooth and fulfilling during those six and a half months. We formed close bonds with several families, including the Topka family, their daughter Marianne, and their son-in-law Wolfgang. They often invited us to their home, and these gatherings were filled with laughter, stories, and shared experiences. Despite our differences, we found common ground in respect, hard work, and family values. My wife's support during this time was invaluable. She adapted to the new environment with grace and curiosity, embracing the challenges and joys of living in a foreign country.

Plate 31
Celebrating Christmas with Marianne and Wolfgang at their residence, 1977

A memorable incident with Marianne's family highlighted the deep-rooted punctuality and discipline in German culture. We were invited to Marianne's parents' house for a gathering. Arriving five minutes early, Marianne informed us that her mother would not appreciate our early arrival. We spent those five minutes outside, ensuring we entered precisely on time. This small act of punctuality was met with warm appreciation from the Topka family, reinforcing the cultural values I had come to admire.

Punctuality extended beyond social gatherings to every aspect of German life, including traffic. Germans strictly adhered to traffic rules, calmly stopping at red lights even when no one was watching, a stark contrast to the often chaotic traffic in India. This disciplined approach left a lasting impression on me.

An Instance of Precision: Our London Consulate Appointment

One vivid memory is the day we visited the consulate for a visa appointment to travel to London. We had scheduled an appointment for 8:00 AM, a time given to us by the consulate officer. Understanding the importance of punctuality and knowing we had to find our way on foot, we left well in advance.

We started our journey from home, strolling through scenic streets with eagerness to arrive on time. The consulate was about a mile away, so we took our time, enjoying the walk and exploring the surroundings. Arriving about ten minutes early, we took a final look around before heading inside.

The waiting hall had a few other people, quietly waiting for their turn. With a mix of anticipation and nervousness, I approached the counter and informed the officer of our appointment with 'Madam'. The officer asked, "Do you have an appointment?" I confidently replied, "Yes, we do." He instructed us to wait on the sofa while he called 'Madam' from the back office.

As we settled in, I noticed the room's atmosphere, typical for a place where important decisions and approvals are made. Soon enough, 'Madam' arrived and called my name. As we approached the counter, I saw the wall clock showed exactly 8:00 AM. She remarked, "You are so punctual."

This compliment brought a sense of pride and a smile to my face. Punctuality had always been a part of my character, something I valued deeply. My German friends often complimented me, saying that I was always a step ahead, even more punctual than they were. This instance at the consulate was a small yet significant testament to the value of punctuality. It reinforced my belief in being timely and how it reflects on one's character.

Strengthening the Bond: Discovering Life Together

As newlyweds, the excitement and joy of discovering life together in a foreign land were both thrilling and enriching. Germany, with its disciplined yet warm culture, became the backdrop for our early years of marriage. These were days of shared dreams and simple pleasures, where every moment seemed filled with promise and happiness. We meticulously planned our time, cherishing every opportunity to explore our new surroundings.

I would come home from the institute, often greeted by the aroma of delicious snacks that my wife had lovingly prepared. These small gestures of care and affection made our home a space of comfort and joy.

Our evenings were often spent together in Hannover's city centre, where we would stroll through bustling streets, enjoy a cup of coffee or tea, and immerse ourselves in the vibrant local culture. Our home and my institute were in opposite directions, but we found a smart solution to this logistical challenge. My wife would come halfway from home, and I would come from the institute, and we would meet in the heart of the city. These journeys through Hannover became cherished memories, with picturesque squares and cosy cafés serving as our meeting spots, where we would share stories of our day, plan for the future, and simply enjoy each other's company.

The Black Fur Coat

I recall an instance when my wife saw a black fur overcoat she admired while strolling the streets. Though it was more expensive than others, it was also more beautiful. She bought it for 100 Marks (the German currency at the time). She wore the same coat on 31st December, 1977, when we returned to India. The black fur coat, with the same charm, remains a cherished possession of my elder daughter.

The Frozen Maschsee Lake (A serene yet vibrant place):

From August to October, Germany's weather was at its most inviting, neither too hot nor too cold, but just perfect for long walks and outdoor activities. We took full advantage of this friendly climate, exploring parks,

Plate 32
Myself and my wife, Krishna, enjoying the winter vibes in heavy snow at Andreasberg, near Hannover.

Plate 33
Spending an evening together near the Maschee lake, the largest artificial lake in Hannover. In winters when the lake would freeze, we would even enjoy walking on it.

visiting local markets, and occasionally venturing into the countryside. The rest of the year, though characterised by shorter days and less sunlight, never deterred our enthusiasm. During winters, when the temperature fell below 10 degree centigrade, the local Maschsee Lake would freeze. It was a pleasure to walk on this long and beautiful lake. When the thickness of the ice exceeded to a certain extent, the authorities allowed sports activities too on it, like ice skating and ice hockey. We have also seen four wheelers (Jeep) running on it. It used to be a place of recreation and entertainment with a big crowd around giving a feel of a fest. The Maschsee Lake Festival is another famous event still celebrated in the month of July-August in Hannover. Germans are known for their resilience and dedication, and we too embraced this ethos. Whether it was rain or shine, work continued uninterrupted, and so did our adventures.

The Unpredictable Weather & the Forgotten Umbrella

Germany's unpredictable weather made a folding umbrella essential. I recall an instance of my initial days there, when I was carrying shopping bags full of winter wear and groceries and lost my way to the institute guest house. Suddenly, snowfall began. Stranded without an umbrella and occupied with bags, I was rescued by local police who, despite the language barrier, managed to get me to my destination.

This experience underscored the importance of carrying an umbrella at all times. In fact, I still have one of the umbrellas from that era, a memento of those early days, symbolising our readiness to face any storm together! My elder daughter recently took the same umbrella on a family trip to Singapore.

I am meticulous in certain aspects of life, a trait that perhaps grew stronger during our time in Germany. This meticulousness is not about being strict or overly fastidious but is simply part of who I am. I balance discipline with joy and light-heartedness. Life in Germany taught us the importance of this balance, with its work ethic characterised by efficiency and precision deeply influencing me.

Waving Goodbye to Germany: Lebewohl

In December 1977, our time in Germany came to an end, and we prepared to return to India. Our Institute Director, Prof. (Dr.) E.G. Niemann came to Hannover airport with a bouquet in his hands and an infectious smile on his face to bid us farewell.

These three years, including the six and a half months with my wife, had been a period of growth and discovery. We had built a home, forged lasting friendships, and created memories that would stay with us forever. Returning to India was bittersweet. While we were leaving behind a life we had come to love, we looked forward to the future in our homeland. The experiences and lessons from Germany had given us a new perspective and a deeper respect for different cultures.

Those early months of our marriage in Germany were filled with learning, growth, and mutual support. We faced challenges together, celebrated victories, and built a foundation of trust and love that would support us through the years to come.

As we stepped into the next phase of our lives, we carried with us the spirit of Germany, celebrating discipline, respect, and the joy of living. Germany became an integral part of our story.

Chapter 8

A Joyous Return: Homecoming with Gifts & Tokens of Affection

Returning to India in December 1977, after our memorable time in Germany, was a bittersweet experience filled with excitement and a touch of sadness at leaving behind a place that had given us so much.

I had spent three years there, including six and a half months with my wife, building a life, creating memories, and immersing ourselves in the rich cultural fabric of Germany. But the joy of returning to our roots and the warm embrace of family was unparalleled.

I come from a large family, seven siblings, each with their own families and even grandchildren. The prospect of reuniting with them was exhilarating.

My wife and I had carefully chosen gifts for every member of our extended family, including elders, siblings, friends, youngsters, and even toddlers. We brought back a variety of items, trying to do justice to each age group. There were shirts, ties, pens, rechargeable torches, mixers, wristwatches, shaving razors, perfumes,

Plate 34
Embracing my dear niece Alka after returning from West Germany

lipsticks, frocks, pullovers, coats, dolls, toy trains, umbrellas, and even sarees and other little trinkets that we thought would bring smiles to their faces.

I remember my wife and I making a list of around 55 people while selecting the gifts so that no one was missed. We planned to bring more than two gifts on average for each person, ensuring everyone felt remembered and cherished.

We were truly blessed to have such a big, bonded, and beautiful family waiting for us back home. Everyone appreciated our thoughtfulness and was amazed at how it was possible to plan and execute so much in just six and a half months of our stay in Germany after marriage, along with my wife settling into the new culture and my professional commitments. This was a way of sharing a piece of our German life with them, and these thoughtful gestures are still fondly remembered by our family today.

One of the most memorable moments of our return was at the airport. Among the many items we brought back was a charming doll, a souvenir that still holds a place in our home. As we stood near the conveyor belt waiting for our luggage, my parents and in-laws watched us from a distance. My wife, carrying the doll in her arms, looked as if she was holding a baby. The sight caused a wave of astonishment among our parents and in-laws, who stood there bewildered, wondering how on earth we could have had a baby in just six and a half months! Their surprise turned into hearty laughter as they approached us and realised that the 'baby' was, in fact, a doll. It was a lighthearted and joyous reunion, setting the tone for the celebrations and homecomings that followed.

Our return was more than just a physical journey; it was a re-immersion into our family life. We had been away, but the love and warmth of our family had remained constant. Each member welcomed us with open arms, eager to hear about our experiences and adventures in a foreign land. The gifts we distributed were received with delight, but it was the stories, shared moments, and laughter that truly mattered.

Living in Germany taught us many things, but it was our family in India that reminded us of the importance of roots and the bonds that hold us together no matter where life takes us. Each sibling, niece, and nephew had grown a bit in our absence, but the essence of our connection remained unchanged.

One particularly touching moment was when I handed a gift to my eldest brother. He looked at the neatly wrapped package, a shirt I had picked out specifically for him, and I could see the happiness on his face.

Settling back into life in India brought its own set of challenges and joys. The bustling streets, the familiar sounds and smells, the chaos and beauty of it all; it was, after all, our home.

One of the most rewarding aspects of our return was sharing our experiences with the younger members of our family. Our nieces and nephews were particularly curious about life in Germany. They would gather around us, wide-eyed and eager, as we recounted tales of our adventures, the cultural differences, and the lessons learned. It felt good to inspire them, to plant seeds of curiosity and ambition in their young minds.

We also brought back traditions and practices that had become a part of our lives in Germany. Celebrating Indian festivals with a touch of German efficiency became a new norm. Reflecting on our homecoming, I realise how those three years in Germany were more than just a chapter in our lives; they were a transformative experience. They shaped our perspectives, broadened our horizons, and made us appreciate the depth of our roots. Coming back to India, we brought with us not just souvenirs and stories but a renewed sense of belonging and purpose.

The laughter at the airport over the doll, the heartfelt welcome, the shared meals and the joyous reunions; all these moments stitched together the fabric of our life.

Settling back in India after experiencing life in Germany was a transition. The disciplined lifestyle and cultural nuances of Germany had left a mark on us, and we were eager to blend those experiences with the warmth and vibrancy of Indian life. Our family played a crucial role in this transition, making us feel at home and helping us adapt to the changes.

> *"Amidst the hustle and bustle, each gift becomes a cherished memory."*

It was a time of reconnecting, sharing, and creating new memories; a beautiful blend of our experiences abroad and the cherished traditions of our homeland.

Chapter 9

Partners in Adventure: Into Nigeria and the Heart of Africa

Returning to India from Germany felt like stepping back into a familiar yet evolving world. After settling down for six months, an unexpected opportunity arose, an invitation to Nigeria in June 1978. We had little knowledge about its geography or the routes the airlines took.

In those days, it was rare for Indians to venture into Africa; Europe and the West were the usual destinations. But I took a chance, buoyed by my adventurous spirit and the support of my wife. She was incredibly supportive, and her cooperative spirit was a great encouragement. She has always been my pillar, supporting my decisions even today. She said, "Let's go and see what awaits us." So, with a mix of excitement and uncertainty, we set off for Nigeria.

Our flight was from Delhi to Rome and then from Rome to Kano, a city in Northern Nigeria, the second largest after Lagos, from where we took another flight to Maiduguri, the capital of the northeastern state of Borno.

Nigeria, the largest country in Africa in terms of population, was both intriguing and daunting.

Upon arrival in Nigeria, we were greeted by a scene that contrasted sharply with our experiences in Germany and India. The state of affairs at the airport alone was surprising. The atmosphere was chaotic, and the unfamiliar faces and the new environment were initially overwhelming.

My wife vividly remembers our first steps in Nigeria and the initial chaos we encountered. Initially, the adjustment was challenging. The climate, the people, and the environment were so different from what we were used to. There were moments of doubt and homesickness. The locals seemed intimidating at first due to cultural differences, and we had to get used to the new lifestyle. However, over time, we adapted and embraced the challenge. I joined the Department of Crop Science in the Faculty of Agriculture at the University of Maiduguri as Lecturer One.

A Decade in Nigeria: Building Agricultural Education

Nigeria, the most populous country in Africa, presented a unique challenge and opportunity. I was the fourth person to join the Faculty of Agriculture. Our mission was monumental; we were to establish the Faculty of Agriculture from the ground up. My role was crucial as I was responsible for setting up the entire course syllabus and initiating the teaching program. I started as a Lecturer One, and during my ten-year tenure, I received two promotions, one to Senior Lecturer and the other to Reader.

Plate 35
Teaching Faculty and BSc Students; Department of Crop Science, Faculty of Agriculture, University of Maiduguri, Nigeria (1983).

We arrived in June, and by October, we had started the academic program. Initially, we focused on basic courses for the B.Sc. level, but within a decade, we expanded to guiding M.Sc. students as well. One incident stands out as a testament to our hard work and dedication.

We had our first batch of M.Sc. students, and their theses needed external evaluation. The external examiner was a prominent professor from the prestigious Ahmadu Bello University, Zaria, Kaduna State, a highly respected institution. I was apprehensive about the evaluation process as it was my first experience guiding a student at this level. I was anxious about his assessment, knowing it would reflect on our fledgling program.

To my relief and pride, he was thoroughly impressed. After reviewing the thesis and the subsequent viva voce of my student, he asked for a copy to take back with him. His appreciation gave me immense satisfaction and a profound sense of accomplishment. It was a significant affirmation that we were on the right track.

Living conditions were another challenge. The university provided accommodation, but there were limited houses on campus. Many employees, including myself, had to live in rented houses off-campus. My first accommodation was quite remote, which was a concern as my wife was expecting our first daughter. I was worried about leaving her alone in a remote location. After expressing my concerns to the administration, they offered us another house, but it was still in an undesirable area.

Plate 36
Experimental Plots in the University of Maiduguri (Nigeria) for Students Field Research (1980)

Plate 37a & 37b
Engaged in Field work and Research with my BSc Student in Maiduguri (1980)

Plate 38
Convocation in the University of Maiduguri, Borno State, Nigeria. Myself along with other colleagues, participating as a Senator

I requested a change once more, which initially upset the housing officials. They warned me that repeated requests would not be entertained. However, my persistence paid off, and on the third attempt, we were given a house off-campus but on the main road, which was much more convenient and safer.

These experiences in Nigeria, from the academic advancements to personal challenges, were instrumental in shaping my career and personal life. The journey was filled with learning, growth, and significant milestones that contributed to my development as an educator and as an individual.

> *"Life's true adventure lies in embracing the unknown and thriving amidst challenges."*

Political Shifts in Nigeria: A Year of Uncertainty and my brief Meeting with General Obasanjo

In 1978, Nigeria was under military rule. General Olusegun Obasanjo was at the helm, and the country was divided into various states, each governed by military officials. Obasanjo had promised to transition power to a civilian government through elections, a promise that seemed almost unbelievable in the African context, where military rule was prevalent. Scepticism was high among the local populace, with many doubting that the military would relinquish control.

Remarkably, however, Obasanjo kept his word and handed over power to a civilian government in 1979, a rare occurrence in the region. Nigeria had been ruled by the military from 1966 to 1999, except for this short period of democracy. During this significant political shift, a celebration was held at our university, attended by various dignitaries, including General Obasanjo himself.

I distinctly remember meeting him in person, shaking hands with him, and engaging in meaningful conversation. He expressed his appreciation for the contributions of Indians in Nigeria, acknowledging our services and expressing his gratitude. Words of appreciation reaffirmed the importance of our presence and efforts in the country. This meeting was a memorable event, especially considering that Obasanjo later became the president of Nigeria as a civilian leader.

As for our living conditions, we had accepted a house off-campus. It was a period filled with anticipation and uncertainty due to the upcoming elections. Many locals were anxious about the outcome, fearing potential violence and bloodshed, which was not uncommon in such transitions. This general sense of unease was palpable, and we too shared these concerns.

Adding to the tension was the existence of a small, mysterious group known as the Metarsine. This group was feared for their alleged practice of sucking human blood, a notion that added an eerie layer of anxiety to an already uncertain time. The fear of what the Metarsine might do during this politically volatile period was ever-present in our minds. The location where we lived in northeastern Nigeria had a relatively better law and order situation compared to the southern regions, where armed robbery was rampant.

The transition from military to civilian government brought hope, but also a fair share of political instability. After four years under civilian rule, political unrest resurfaced, adding to the uncertainty of life in Nigeria.

Later in 1983, the military took over the civilian government again. During such a particularly tumultuous period, I was given the responsibility to take my students on a study tour across the southern part of Nigeria. It was a time of great uncertainty.

Despite the risks, I had to fulfil my responsibility. As we travelled, locals questioned our journey, concerned for our safety. Their warnings were a stark reminder of the volatile situation. Instructions for children were clear—to maintain composure and avoid any provocative actions. I remember an incident where we had taken two buses full of students on a tour. At one point, while setting up barricades, a military officer halted our bus due to a comment made by a local student in their native language. The officer's demeanour was intense, signalling that any misstep could lead to unforeseen consequences. This incident emphasised the need for strict adherence to instructions to ensure everyone's safety and avoid escalating tensions in such a volatile environment.

Living through this period in Nigeria was a mix of historical significance and personal challenges. The transition of power from military to civilian rule was a landmark event, and being a part of it, albeit indirectly, was an experience that underscored the unpredictable nature of political landscapes in developing nations.

Struggles and Joys: Life in Nigeria

In our off-campus house in Nigeria, we faced numerous challenges. The house was large but lacked consistent utilities. The electricity supply was erratic, often coming and going without warning. Water was another significant issue; the supply was irregular, and we frequently found ourselves without any.

To cope with this, I developed a routine. I would wake up early in the morning, taking empty jerrycans to the university in my car to fill them with water. This daily routine became one of my primary concerns, but somehow, time passed, and we adapted. I repeated this process in the afternoon to ensure we had enough water for our daily needs. Regularly, I visited the electricity and water boards to plead for a more reliable supply, but the situation remained unpredictable.

Living in a large house without reliable electricity and water was tough, but we managed to make do. The experience taught us resilience and adaptability, qualities that have stayed with us ever since. Despite the difficulties, we cherished the moments of joy and the small victories in our daily struggle to maintain a semblance of normalcy.

Birth of Our First Child: Embracing Parenthood

Despite these hardships, life went on. During this period, on 23rd July, 1979, our first daughter, Sangita, was born, bringing immense joy to our lives. However, her birth coincided with the holiday season, and most of our Indian acquaintances, with whom we had developed close relationships over the past year, had returned to India for the holidays.

This left us with a minimal support network, making the situation even more difficult. A couple from Delhi, the Sondhis, who became our friends in Nigeria, were of great help at this time. Mrs. Sushma Sondhi stayed with my wife throughout her labour and delivery. The nurse who attended to my wife was an Irish lady, and her care was also a source of comfort during this time.

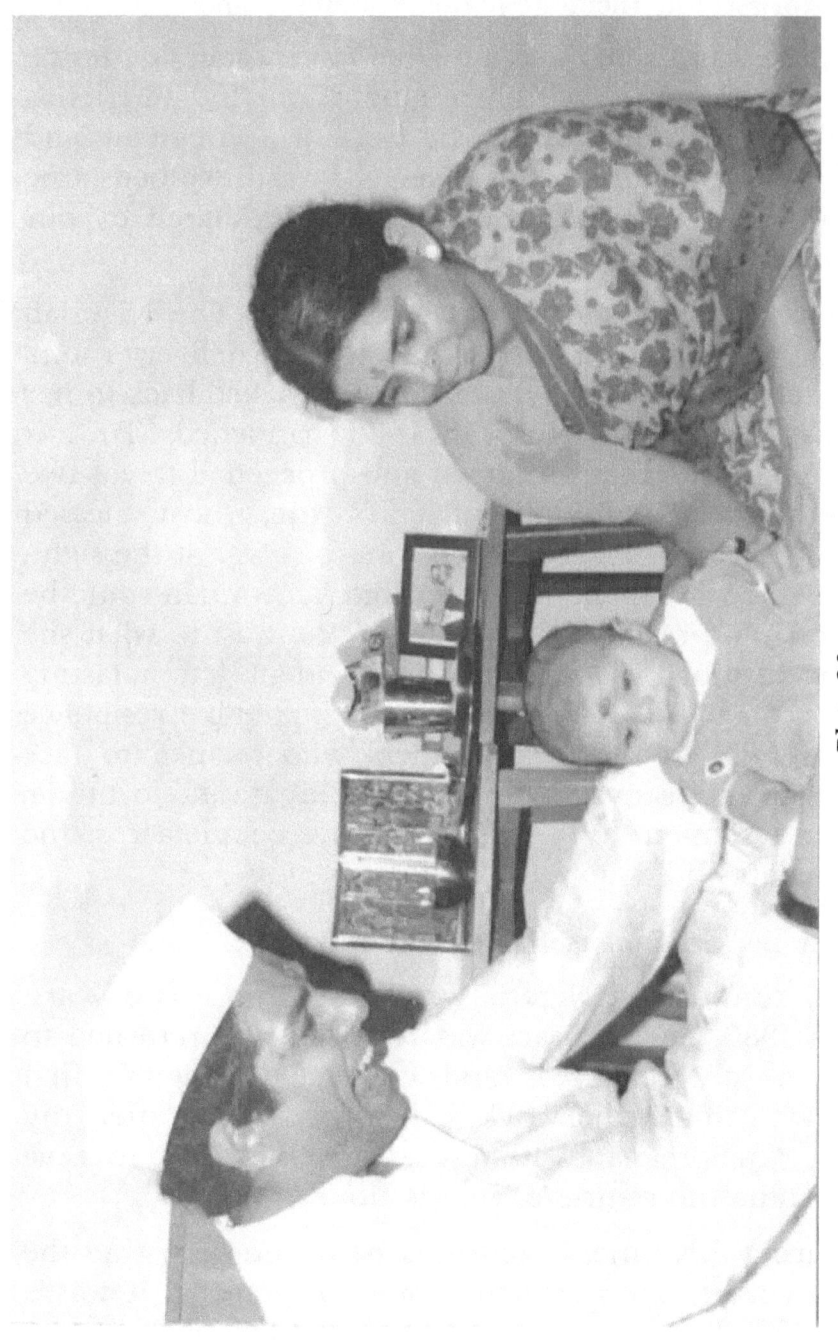

Plate 39
Celebrating our little daughter Sangita's first Diwali in Nigeria, October 20, 1979

An Unforgettable Incident at the Nursing Home

There was a remarkable incident at the nursing home where our daughter was born. One of our Indian friends was there with his wife, who was also pregnant and admitted in the same room. The room had two beds, one with my wife and the other temporarily shared by our Indian acquaintance and a Nigerian woman.

What happened next was astonishing. The Nigerian woman, who was in labour, was taken to the delivery room. After delivering her baby, she casually walked back to her bed as if nothing significant had happened. To our amazement, she then sat down and proceeded to eat two whole chickens. Our Indian friend's wife, who witnessed this, was utterly shocked. She began to shiver at the sight, unable to comprehend how the Nigerian woman could be so strong and resilient. It was a stark contrast to what she was accustomed to seeing. This incident left a lasting impression on us. It highlighted the incredible resilience and strength of the local women, who seemed to face childbirth and recovery with remarkable ease and fortitude. It was a testament to the different ways people across the world adapt and endure the challenges of life.

Coming Back to India: Birth of Our Son

My contracts in Nigeria were typically for two years, and in 1980, our contract was renewed. We returned to India in July that year and celebrated Sangita's first birthday, bringing her back to her roots. Soon after, my wife became pregnant with our second child. I had to leave her in India and return to Nigeria alone.

During this time, I secured a better house within the campus, a beautiful structure built by Italians. It was a wonderful place, a stark contrast to our previous

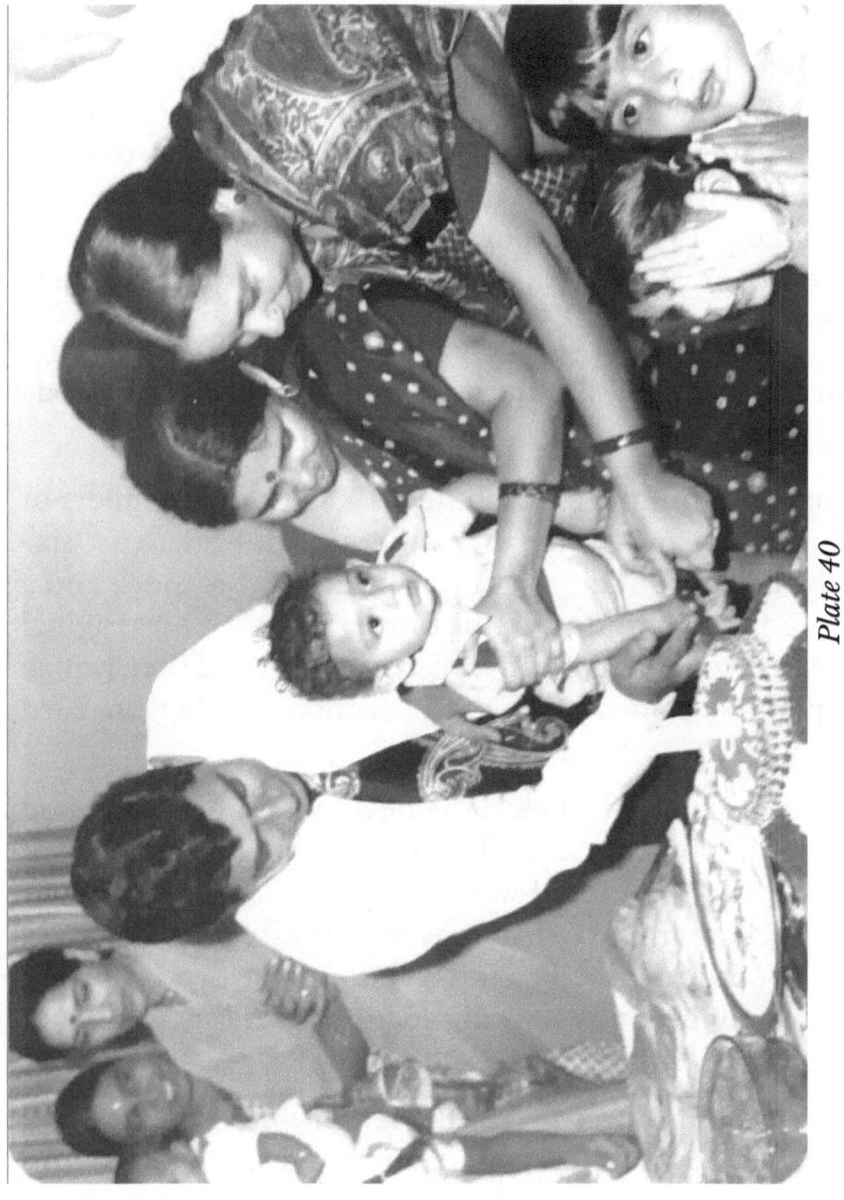

Plate 40
Celebrating our son, Ankur's first birthday with Indian friends, at our residence in Nigeria, 21st January, 1982

accommodations, a home that felt like a mini-castle to us, as our children still recall. I felt proud to call it our home, where our children could thrive.

In late January 1981, I received a telegram from my father-in-law with the message "Blessed with a son." I was thrilled, elated, and happy. In July 1981, I came back to India after the birth of our son, Ankur Sharma, who was born on 21st January, 1981, in Jaipur. I then brought my wife and children back to Nigeria, where we settled into our new home.

Celebrating Sangita's Birthday Amidst the Historical Flood of 1981

I arrived in India on 20th July, 1981. Many members of my family, including my wife, elder daughter Sangita, six-month-old son Ankur, my eldest sister, my brothers, and a few more, had come to Delhi to receive me. Our original plan was to remain in Delhi for a day or two and then return to Jaipur to celebrate Sangita's second birthday on 23rd July.

Unfortunately, we heard the news of an unprecedented flood in Jaipur on 22nd July, following three days of nonstop rains. The flood was so heavy that Jaipur, after its establishment in 1727, had never witnessed such havoc. These floods, described as the worst in over two centuries, transformed the landscape, inundating areas that had never seen such devastation before.

The underground petrol tanks at filling stations were carried away by the flood and later found some kilometres away. With roads and rail lines submerged, my father-in-law told us that it was impossible to reach Jaipur. At the Jaipur Airport, the runway was covered with

Plate no. 41
Sangita's second birthday celebration in New Delhi amidst the historical flood of 1981 (23rd July)

a foot of mud and sand. Undeterred, we adapted to the situation, choosing to celebrate our daughter's special day in Delhi itself, surrounded by the warmth of family and friends.

As conditions in Jaipur gradually improved, we seized an opportunity to reach there by train and then by jeep, navigating through a landscape scarred by floodwaters and reconstruction. It was a testament to human resilience and determination, overcoming nature's fury to reach our destination.

Finally, we could reunite with my parents and other family members who had weathered the storm. After about three months, we came back to Nigeria, this time in the new house 'R-8'.

"In the midst of chaos, there is also opportunity."

– Sun Tzu

The Cherished Memories of R-8: Our Minicastle

This was a very good accommodation within the university campus. Once we secured proper housing within the campus, life became significantly smoother. The new house had reliable electricity and water, which eased many of our daily struggles. This improvement in living conditions brought a sense of relief and stability, especially for my wife.

Sangita still fondly remembers the house. She often says it looked like a castle, with its duplex structure, high ceiling, big staircase, long windows on the sides, and a vast ground in front surrounded by a green hedge marking the boundary of the premises. The land behind the house was lush with trees, adding to its charm.

On the ground floor, there was a drawing room, a dining area, a spacious kitchen, a big storeroom, a backyard, and a garage with a shutter door. There were three bedrooms on the first floor, with spacious washrooms with bathtubs and a balcony.

We still remember the variety of delicious recipes prepared by my wife, the birthday parties, and the social gatherings, which were a part of our life here. As I also had some experience in cooking from my Udaipur and Germany days, I applied my skills too. The days I prepared pizzas in our oven became special celebrations for our family, still fondly remembered as 'Pizza Party'. My wife would be relieved from the kitchen, I would take charge, and the children would be excited to apparently assist me, by just being around and listening to my stories while cooking. The children still remember the fun they used to have, climbing on the grill doors in the backyard, the bedtime prayers they used to say, climbing trees, running around and the playtime in the evenings.

There was a family from a nearby country, Chad, who lived in our servant quarters. Saale, along with his wife Maathe, younger brother Bukol, and six children, lived in the quarters. The three younger ones were born during our stay there. Saale worked in the same University of Maiduguri as a painter, his wife used to sell fritters roadside, and Bukol, a person around six and a half feet tall, helped us with our household chores. Sangita and Ankur used to have company playing with his children and still count their names on their fingers: Selu, Laadi, Kaati, Chiwane Fambo, and Anjani.

Plate 42
Our Car, Volkswagen Beetle: A Symbol of Our Journey in Nigeria.
Sangita and Ankur waiting to be dropped at school.

In my study on the first floor, I had a typewriter, which I had bought from Singapore in 1982. It was considered a privilege to have one in those days, and I remember having typed so many letters and other official documents on it.

Volkswagen Beetle: A Symbol of Our Journey in Nigeria

I fondly remember our Volkswagen Beetle, a white car numbered 'BO 6017 MA' that became a significant part of our lives. Let me take you back to 30th June, 1978, when I first arrived in Nigeria. Getting accustomed to life there was quite an adventure.

It took about 15–20 days for our car to arrive; the agent had to coordinate with the university for the delivery. It wasn't something we were used to back then. We bought it for 3,800 Naira, and after ten years, in September 1988, as we prepared to leave, we sold it for hardly 4,000 Naira. The car was a symbol of our journey, carrying countless memories.

Children's Primary Education:

Nigeria, with its contrasts and challenges, became our home. The educational system there was commendable, and our children's schooling proceeded smoothly. The International Primary School of Maiduguri, situated on a campus close to our house, was excellent. Sangita and Ankur attended this school, which had a significant number of expatriate children.

The vice chancellor's daughter, Habiba, and my daughter were friends. The school had a diverse mix of students from different socio-cultural and geographic backgrounds. Most of them were from economically well-off families. The principal, Ms. King, hailed from the

Plate no. 43
The International Primary School at the University of Maiduguri campus, from where Sangita (sitting third from the left in the front row) and Ankur received their primary education.

West Indies. Her name, which we playfully translated to "Kumari Raja" in Hindi, became a source of harmless fun among the Indian community. Sangita's class teacher, Mrs. Sanusi, was a gentle and smart lady from the nearby country of Ghana. School days in Nigeria were a blend of education and cultural exposure. The children sang the national anthem during assembly and had glimpses into Christianity, enriching their understanding of different cultures.

Absences and Missed Occasions:

Living in Nigeria for ten years shaped us in many ways. The cultural differences were vast yet enriching. Being there for around a decade was a transformative experience, both professionally and personally. During this time, many significant events occurred in India, and unfortunately, we couldn't be there for most of them. The challenges of communication and transportation made it difficult to stay connected with our family back home. Despite these obstacles, we managed to maintain a semblance of connection through letters and occasional visits.

While we were building a life in Nigeria, my brothers and sisters got married. Two of my brothers' weddings happened without my presence, a fact that still tugs at my heart. Similarly, I missed my two brothers-in-law's and one sister-in-law's weddings. The inability to attend these family milestones was a heavy price to pay for our expatriate life.

One of the most painful absences was during my father-in-law's demise. By the time we received the information, it was too late to make any travel arrangements. In those days, the concept of instant communication was a distant dream. Letters took 15 to 20 days to reach their destination, and sometimes, they wouldn't even arrive.

The birth of our first daughter, Sangita, and every significant detail about her was communicated through letters. These letters were our lifeline, our only way to share our joys and sorrows with our families. Despite the uncertainty of their arrival, we continued to write, clinging to this fragile thread of connection.

Whenever we planned a visit to India, it required meticulous planning and early reservations. Booking seats for our journey had to be done four months in advance. The lack of a robust communication system made these trips even more challenging. The process of securing travel arrangements was cumbersome, reflecting the broader communication issues we faced regularly.

Memories with My Younger Brother, Subhash:

The years spent in Nigeria were transformative and full of memorable moments. A significant chapter of our lives unfolded when my younger brother, Dr. Subhash Chandra Sharma, joined us in 1982. He joined as a teacher at Borno Teacher's College, Ministry of Education. His arrival brought a wave of familial warmth and camaraderie that enriched our stay.

Having Subhash with us was a source of immense joy. His presence turned our daily routines into cherished memories. We cooked meals together, celebrated birthdays, and even cut each other's hair. The laughter and conversations we shared during these simple activities strengthened our bond and created a sense of home away from home.

Plate 44
Family photograph with my younger brother Dr Subhash Chandra Sharma, on the occasion of Rakshabandhan, in Nigeria, 1983. At the time Subhash was also working in a college in Maiduguri.

My nephew, Pranay Sharma, was born in Nigeria on 25th February, 1983. Watching my nephew grow was a special experience that added another layer of happiness to our lives. Today, Pranay lives in Dubai, but the memories of his early years in Nigeria remain close to our hearts. It was a pleasant coincidence that many years later, when my son Ankur was working in Dubai, Pranay also moved there, and they both lived together for a few years, creating similar beautiful memories.

Birth of My Younger Daughter:

In August 1984, I travelled to India with my family. This time, I stayed for about four months and returned to Nigeria alone in October, leaving my wife and children with my parents. She was expecting our third child. On 2nd January, 1985, our younger daughter, Gunjan Sharma, was born in Jaipur.

A few months later, in April 1985, I returned to India and brought my wife, son, and two daughters back to Nigeria. Our journey took us through Zurich, Switzerland, where, due to the extreme cold, a few-month-old Gunjan started turning blue, and we had to wrap her up in multiple warm layers.

Social Life: Seeking Indian Roots in a Foreign Land

There were many Indian families in the city and in the university campus too. In the evenings, after dinner, a few families would walk around the campus and engage in light conversation. My younger daughter, Gunjan, who was around three years old, would often get tired midway, and I had to carry her on my shoulders for the rest of the walk. Yet the next day, she would insist on coming along, promising not to give up walking midway, only to repeat

Plate 45
Myself with my three children; Sangita, Ankur and Gunjan at our residence in Maiduguri, 1986. My wife is obviously missing in this family picture as she is the one clicking it.

the cycle of getting tired and being carried on my shoulders again. There were families from different parts of India, representing different religions and regions, yet all were united in a foreign land with the strong bond of being Indian.

Festivals like Diwali and other significant occasions such as Independence and Republic Day were celebrated with great enthusiasm within the Indian community. Once on August 15, I attended the celebration in a traditional attire, white *'Dhoti Kurta'* and a *'Gandhi Topi'*, which was well appreciated. We also organised picnics. I recall one of these at a place called New Marte near a lake, where around 15–20 Indian families gathered and enjoyed a wonderful time. Our trips to Yankari Wildlife Park and the town of Mubi with friends were also memorable.

Among our friends were Dr. U.C. Shukla, who had been my teacher in Udaipur for a short period and later became the Dean of the Faculty of Agriculture in Nigeria. I have always been fortunate to have good people cross my path, providing valuable academic and personal support.

Another friend was Dr. U.C. Pandey from Hisar, who was the vegetable seed production specialist in our department. Yet another couple, with whom we played bridge on weekends, was Dr. Sahay and his wife, both anaesthetists at the Medical College. The Sondhi couple from Delhi, working at Federal College at the time, is now settled in the US and still in contact with us.

My wife found solace and joy in participating in religious activities with the Indian community in Nigeria. She regularly attended bhajans and other religious

Plate 46
Myself in traditional Indian attire with Dr. U.C. Shukla and his family. He had been my teacher in Udaipur for a short period and later became the Dean of the Faculty of Agriculture in Nigeria.

gatherings like *'Satyanarayanji Ki Katha,'* which provided a sense of cultural continuity and spiritual comfort. These activities were a crucial part of her life, helping her stay connected to her roots and cope with the challenges of living in a foreign land.

Professionally, my tenure in Nigeria was deeply fulfilling. Establishing the Faculty of Agriculture at the University of Maiduguri from scratch was a monumental task. We developed the agricultural curriculum, starting from BSc courses and eventually expanding to MSc programs. One of my students, after completing BSc from our department, went to the USA for MSc and Phd, and later came back to join us as faculty.

Letter from Dr M.S. Swaminathan, Director General of Indian Council of Agricultural Research (ICAR) : A testament to my Academic Achievements

I was extremely happy to receive a letter from Dr M. S. Swaminathan, who at that time was the Director General of Indian Council of Agricultural Research (ICAR) & Secretary to the Government of India. He appreciated my work in Nigeria and also asked me to share any information or material which might be of value to the green revolution back in India.

My Nigerian team's contributions were instrumental in this endeavour. They travelled to India multiple times to recruit talented individuals for the development of Nigeria's agricultural sector and educational infrastructure. Their efforts played a significant role in building a robust faculty and advancing agricultural education in the region.

Plate 47
Correspondence letter to me in Nigeria, from Dr M S Swaminathan, the Director General of Indian Council of Agricultural Research (ICAR), Krishi Bhavan, New Delhi

Wrapping up the Nigerian Decade: Bidding Adieu

In August 1988, we prepared to return to India permanently. The process of winding up our life in Nigeria was filled with mixed emotions. Selling our beloved Volkswagen Beetle was a poignant moment, symbolising the end of an era. The car had been an integral part of our lives, carrying countless memories of our journeys and experiences.

As we were wrapping up our stay, an unfortunate incident occurred. My daughter Sangita fractured her hand while playing and jumping from a tree in our backyard. The absence of our car, which we had already sold, made the situation more stressful. However, the Indian community stepped in to help. They assisted us in transporting my daughter to the hospital and ensured we had the support we needed during this challenging time. A kind-hearted Pakistani doctor attended to my daughter, confirming that it was a complex fracture involving both the long bones of the left forearm and a few small bones of the wrist. The support from our friends and the timely medical care made a difficult situation more manageable. Sangita had to travel back to India in a plaster cast.

Our flight back to India was from Kano to Amsterdam and then Amsterdam to Delhi. We took this opportunity to make a short visit to Germany from Amsterdam. It was exciting to reunite with our old friends, Marianne and Wolfgang, after so many years. This time, our children were new additions to our gathering. Their children, Henrick and Tado, soon became friends with Sangita, Ankur, and Gunjan. We visited a few places, including a zoo that our children enjoyed the most. We still have pictures and videos captured there with our bulky video camera, which recorded on the similarly bulky video cassettes of those times. After reliving our old German memories and creating new ones, we proceeded from Germany to Amsterdam and finally flew to New Delhi.

The memories of our time in Nigeria, especially the years shared with my brother and his family, are precious. The experiences we had, the bonds we strengthened, and the milestones we celebrated together have left an indelible mark on our hearts. Reflecting on our decade in Nigeria, I realise how those years shaped us. The experiences we gathered, the challenges we overcame, and the friendships we formed became integral parts of our lives. We learned to adapt, to find joy in small victories, and to remain connected with our roots despite the distance.

Our house in Nigeria, R8, remains a cherished memory. The Volkswagen Beetle, the vast grounds, the lush trees, the evening walks, and the social gatherings are all part of the vivid recollections of our time there. In retrospect, our ten years in Nigeria were a period of immense growth and learning. We faced challenges, celebrated milestones, and built a life rich with experiences.

My second daughter, Gunjan Sharma, was too young to have strong memories of Nigeria. However, my first daughter, Sangita, holds vivid memories of our time there. My son, Ankur, also had fond recollections, especially of our duplex house, numbered R-8. He used to see live satellite images of R-8 and often thought of visiting Nigeria again to relive those memories. This reflects the impact those years had on our family.

Plate 48
In Germany, our children with Marianne and Wolfgang's children, Henrick and Tado, en route to India, when we finally returned from Nigeria in September, 1988.

Our time in Nigeria was not just about professional achievements but also about personal growth and understanding. We learned to appreciate different cultures, adapt to new environments, and value the simple joys of life. These lessons have stayed with us, influencing our approach to challenges and opportunities alike.

Reflecting on those years, I am filled with gratitude for the experiences and the people who enriched our journey. Despite the distance and the difficulties, we remained connected to our roots and emerged stronger, more resilient, and deeply appreciative of the journey we undertook. My wife's support was instrumental in navigating these adventures. Her resilience and adaptability matched my own, making us a formidable team.

Chapter 10

Wanderlust Chronicles: Eagerness to Explore Cultures and Countries

My journey through life has been marked by remarkable travels across continents, each leaving an indelible impression on my soul.

"The journey through cultures and countries is a testament to the transformative power of embracing the unfamiliar."

- Anonymous

The memories of my travels, particularly during the years I spent in Germany and Nigeria, stand out vividly. My three-year stay in Germany and a decade-long stay in Nigeria were punctuated by biennial trips to India, each lasting a few months. These journeys not only included visits to India but also explorations of various other countries, enriching my life with a multitude of experiences and cultural encounters.

First International Exposure: The Mesmerizing Snowfall in Moscow

In 1974, I embarked on my first international journey aboard Aeroflot, the Soviet Union's airline, bound for Germany with a 24-hour layover in Moscow. It was November, and Moscow was in the grip of its typical freezing cold. It was my first venture outside India, and the experience was unforgettable.

Witnessing snowfall for the first time, I was mesmerised by the delicate white flakes descending from the sky, although the biting cold was unlike anything I had ever experienced. The intensity of the cold drove me back to my hotel room, where I sought refuge under layers of warmth, trying to fend off the shivering chill that seemed to seep into my bones. The next leg of my journey took me from Moscow to Frankfurt. From there, I travelled to Hannover by train, a journey that allowed me to witness the scenic beauty of the German countryside.

My Mentor's Invitation to Germany

Dr. Avatar Krishna Kaul, my mentor during my MSc and PhD, played a pivotal role in my life. He was more than just a teacher; he was a guiding force, a guru in the truest sense. He invited me to Germany for post-doctoral research, and his encouragement opened doors to opportunities that shaped my career and broadened my horizons.

Dr. Kaul, who had a distinguished academic background with a PhD from Canada and post-doctoral work in Australia, brought a wealth of knowledge and experience. I owe much of my professional success to his mentorship.

The Europe Diaries

While residing in Germany, I seized the opportunity to explore numerous European countries. My travels took me to iconic cities such as Warsaw, Paris, London, Amsterdam, Stockholm, Rome, and Zurich, to name a few. Each city offered a unique charm and a distinct cultural flavour.

Warsaw:

In 1976, I attended a scientific conference in Warsaw, Poland, a city that exuded charm and resilience. Its history and culture captivated me and I found myself lost in its beauty. During the 5-day Annual meeting of European Society for New Methods in Agricultural Research (ESNA) (13th-17th September), I presented two original research papers at Warsaw.

Enchanting Paris:

In 1977, Paris enchanted me with its allure. This time, my wife, Krishna was also with me. I marvelled at the Eiffel Tower and immersed myself in the artistic splendour of the Louvre, where I beheld the enigmatic smile of the Mona Lisa. Such is the fame of this enigmatic portrait that it attracts millions, all vying for a glimpse of her elusive smile. My own encounter with this masterpiece was nothing short of mesmerising. Wandering through Montmartre's winding streets, I felt the pulse of bohemian artistry that once thrived in the city's heart.

Voyage Across the Baltic Sea to Sweden:

Later that year, my travels led me to Sweden. The journey began in Kiel, Germany, where we embarked on a ship bound for Gothenburg, Sweden. The voyage across the Baltic Sea was serene, the gentle sway of the ship and the expanse of the open water creating a sense of peaceful

Plate 49
An evening in Paris: Myself and my wife posing in front of the Eiffel Tower, 1977

Plate 50
At the top floor of the Eiffel Tower

Plate no. 51
Louvre Museum, Paris

anticipation. As we approached Gothenburg, the skyline emerged like a watercolour painting, each building and spire reflecting the city's rich history and culture. From Gothenburg, we drove to Uppsala to attend a conference, another Annual meeting of ESNA, where again I got an opportunity to present two of our research papers. I still remember this ride to Uppsala with Professor Niemann, our Director, in his Mercedes. Later, we headed to Stockholm, the beautiful capital of Sweden. Stockholm greeted us with its crisp air and harmonious blend of old-world charm and modern sophistication. Every moment spent there was a feast for the senses.

In Stockholm, I had the honour of visiting the *Konserthuset Stockholm* (the Stockholm Concert Hall), the venue of the Nobel Prize Award Ceremony every year, a place that symbolises the pinnacle of human achievement and intellect. Professor Niemann, who was a well wisher and probably saw some talent and potential in me, jokingly remarked, "Trilok, perhaps one day you will visit this place again to receive a Nobel Prize!" The experience was humbling and inspiring, a reminder of the incredible potential of human endeavour. We wandered through cobblestone streets and explored some historic sites. The memory of Stockholm remains vivid, a testament to the city's charm.

London and Rome:

London's history and grandeur left me in awe, particularly the visit to the Jewel House in the Tower of London, where the sight of the *Kohinoor* diamond, a gem with roots in India, fascinated me. A highlight of London was the visit to Madame Tussauds wax museum, a world unto itself where lifelike sculptures of celebrities and historical figures stood frozen in time. Among these, the

Plate no. 52
With Mahatma Gandhi's wax statue at the Madame Tussauds Museum, London

statue of Mahatma Gandhi was particularly striking. The detail and realism were astonishing, and my wife and I couldn't resist taking pictures with this lifelike representation of the revered leader. The moment captured in a photograph symbolised the enduring influence of Indian values on a global stage, bridging continents and cultures through the lens of history.

I remember a humorous incident at Madame Tussauds where I stood silently like a statue. A few people gathered and even started betting on me being a statue until I blinked my eyes intentionally and smiled, making everyone laugh.

In 1978, while travelling to Nigeria for the first time, our flight took us from Delhi to Rome and then from Rome to Kano, a city in Northern Nigeria. During this journey, we had an opportunity to explore Rome and the Vatican City.

Journey Through Singapore and Bangkok

Travelling with children in the early 1980s presented unique challenges. Seats were scarce, and carrying feeding supplies and other essentials added to the complexity of our journeys.

So, in 1982, when our son was just a year and a half old and Sangita was still very young, we left them with my in-laws in Delhi and embarked on a journey to Bangkok and Singapore. The contrast between the two cities was striking. Bangkok, with its hustle and bustle, felt similar to our own cities, but Singapore left an indelible mark with its unique charm and modernity.

Our first impression of Singapore was fantastic. The Changi Airport, even then, was a marvel. Although it was not fully operational, the sheer scale and vision behind it were impressive. The Singapore government's foresight in developing such infrastructure was evident. Today, Changi Airport is one of the largest and busiest airports in the world.

- **The Snake Charmer's Challenge**

We booked a sightseeing package that took us on a tour bus with people from different nationalities. One of the stops was a small auditorium with a capacity of about a hundred people. There, we were treated to a unique performance by a snake charmer, reminiscent of the ones we used to see in India during our childhood. The charmer played his flute, and the snake danced to its tune, creating a nostalgic yet thrilling atmosphere.

At the end of the performance, the snake charmer invited the audience to come up on stage and have the snake draped around their necks. I knew my wife would never agree to such a thing, so without saying a word, I stood up and fearlessly walked to the stage. The audience clapped as the charmer placed the snake around my neck. It was a unique experience, but as the snake slithered closer to my face, I began to feel a twinge of fear.

"Travelling with open eyes and an open heart unveils the beauty of diversity and the interconnectedness of our world."

- **Capturing the Moment**

On one side of the stage was the snake charmer, and on the other, a photographer with a Polaroid instant camera. He captured the moment, and after the program ended, handed me the photo. That picture became a cherished memory, a tangible reminder of the unique experience we had in Singapore.

Plate 53
The snake charmer's challenge accepted in Singapore; A Python around my neck (1982)

Our trip to Singapore was filled with many such memorable moments. The city's modernity, cleanliness, and the unique experiences it offered left a lasting impression on us. The snake charmer incident was just one of the many adventures we had, and it remains a story I often share with fondness.

I also bought a typewriter from Singapore, which, at the time, was as cutting-edge as the latest iPads today. I used it for many years to type letters and official documents in my study in Nigeria. Eventually, I brought it back to India and later sold it, realising it was no longer practical as technology evolved.

We explored myriad attractions in Singapore, from the lush gardens to the bustling markets of Chinatown and Little India. Every corner of the city offered something new and exciting, making our stay there truly memorable.

Switzerland Trip: The Challenge Amidst the Serenity

In 1985, while bringing our youngest daughter, Gunjan, to Nigeria for the first time from India, we encountered a memorable incident in Zurich. Amidst the chilly weather, Gunjan, who was just a few months old, developed a bluish hue due to the cold. This alarming situation prompted us to swiftly return to the hotel and cover her up in warm layers, ensuring her comfort in the face of unexpected weather conditions.

Such experiences underscored the importance of flexibility and preparedness when raising young children abroad and frequently travelling with them. Every decision was guided by a deep commitment to ensuring our children's safety and happiness, even in unfamiliar surroundings.

Plate 54
Getting on a boat in Amsterdam, The Netherlands, 1976. I went to meet Dr. Sosulski (Dr. Kaul's Ph.D. guide) to explore the opportunity to work in his lab.

Switzerland, with its breathtaking landscapes and serene environment was amazing. The Swiss Alps, with their snow-capped peaks and pristine lakes, evoked a sense of awe and tranquillity. The country's pristine beauty provided a perfect backdrop for reflection and relaxation, leaving me with cherished memories and a deep appreciation for its natural splendour.

Amsterdam and Other Adventures

Amsterdam, the city of canals, has always been one of my favourite destinations. I visited it twice while living in Germany. Later, in 1988, while returning to India after a decade-long stay in Nigeria, I had the opportunity to visit Amsterdam again, this time with my wife and three children.

Throughout my travels, the friendships and connections I forged played a significant role in enriching my experiences. Every year, I made it a point to send New Year and Christmas cards to friends and acquaintances, a tradition that kept me connected with those who mattered to me. I fondly remember using my typewriter to compose these heartfelt messages, each keystroke a testament to the bonds of friendship and the joy of staying connected.

USA & Canada Visit: A Memorable Drive of more than 5000 kms

In April 2016, we travelled to North America (USA and Canada). Our son, Ankur, joined us from Dubai with his wife and daughter. We landed in Boston, where my nephew, Sanket Sharma, warmly welcomed us with his wife Shipra. Sanket, now a Senior Manager in Machine Learning/Artificial Intelligence Product at HP Inc., has recently shifted to Austin, Texas.

After two days, we rented a car, and Ankur drove around 2,500 kilometres in 10 days, covering important places on the East Coast, including Boston, New Jersey, New York, Philadelphia, and Washington, DC. We also visited Harvard University and MIT.

We enjoyed the scenic beauty of Niagara Falls from the US side and then entered Canada to witness the even more beautiful sight of the falls. In Canada, we visited Toronto, Montreal, Ottawa, and other smaller cities along the way while enjoying our car drive. We then returned to Washington, DC, where we surrendered the rented car and flew to Las Vegas, renowned for its casinos and nightlife. We also visited a few casinos and nightclubs after 2 AM in the night.

On the West Coast, we rented another car to visit cities like Los Angeles (through Death Valley) and San Francisco (along the Pacific Coastal Highway No. 101). Ankur, enthusiastic about marathons, found an opportunity to run a half-marathon near Los Angeles (Two Orange County). The drive from San Francisco to Los Angeles was long but enjoyable. We drove through Silicon Valley, home to the world's largest IT companies, and visited the iconic Golden Gate Bridge in San Francisco.

A memorable highlight of our stay in San Francisco was visiting the family of my teacher from IARI, New Delhi, the late Dr. A.K. Kaul. His family resides in San Jose, a town near SFO. Dr Kaul had passed away nearly a decade ago. Along with Mrs Uma Kaul (my Guru Mata), we also met their eldest daughter and son. The younger

Plate 55
My wife Krishna in front of the White House, Washington D.C., during our USA Canada trip with Ankur and his family, 2016

Plate 56
Ankur posing near the Statue of Liberty, New York, 2016

daughter, who lived far away, could not come. Mrs Kaul was very happy to see me with my family. It was a dream come true for me as I had never thought of visiting the USA. It was all due to Ankur, who made it possible. Later, when Mrs Kaul heard the news of the passing away of our son, she contacted me to express her condolences. Her words, "This should not happen even to the enemies," still echo in my mind.

After staying a couple of days in San Francisco, Ankur returned the rented car after driving another 2500 kms over a period of 11-12 days. In May 2016, Ankur and his family returned to Dubai, while my wife and I flew back to India. The vastness and diversity of North America were awe-inspiring, offering experiences ranging from bustling cities to serene natural landscapes. Each city had its unique charm, and the natural wonders left us in awe.

South Africa: A blend of Historical sites and Natural Wonders

South Africa was another highlight of our travels. During our 2017-18 trip to Dubai, Ankur had planned a visit to South Africa. In March 2018, we flew from Dubai to Johannesburg, where Ankur rented a car and drove to Cape Town, visiting various cities along the way. In Johannesburg, we explored Kruger National Park and Soweto in particular.

Ankur ran an ultramarathon in Cape Town, covering 56 kilometres in the Two Oceans Ultra Marathon. My main attractions were:

- The Pietermaritzburg railway station, where Mahatma Gandhi was evicted from a first-class compartment in 1893 due to racial discrimination. The station is still in operation.

- Robben Island Prison in Cape Town, where Nelson Mandela was imprisoned under harsh conditions. The menu for meals was segregated, with inferior quality and quantity for Africans.
- Soweto: The township known for significant uprisings against government policies. Surprisingly, Nelson Mandela's residence is now a museum, and Desmond Tutu's house, opposite Mandela's, is also notable. Both have been awarded the Nobel Peace Prize.

We visited other cities such as Pretoria, Durban, Bloemfontein, East London and Stellenbosch. On 1st April, we flew from Cape Town to Dubai, where Ankur and his family stayed, while my wife and I returned to Jaipur. The country's rich cultural heritage and stunning landscapes were a revelation, offering a blend of historical sites and natural wonders.

A World Explored; A Life Enriched

As I reflect on these journeys, the memories come rushing back, each one vivid and full of life. The excitement of exploring new places, the joy of discovering different cultures, and the thrill of new experiences are integral to our travel adventures. Each trip was a story in itself, filled with moments of wonder and discovery.

Plate 57
A selfie at the Freedom Park, Pretoria, South Africa; March, 2018

Plate 58
At the Blyde River Canyon Nature Reserve, South Africa

Plate 59
Bourke's Luck Potholes, famous for iconic, spectacular viewpoints

Plat 60
Myself riding an ostrich in South Africa

Plate 61
Boarding the Aerial Cable way to have a view of the picturesque Table Mountain ,Cape Town.

Travelling broadens one's perspective, opens up new horizons, and creates lasting memories. The experiences we had, the people we met, and the places we visited have all left an indelible mark on our lives. As I recount these memories, I am filled with gratitude for the opportunities I've had and the journeys I've embarked upon. Each place holds a piece of my heart, a testament to the transformative power of travel.

"Travelling is not just about seeing new places; it's about becoming part of their stories and leaving a piece of ourselves behind."

Chapter 11

Krishna, My Dear Wife: The Backbone of My Life

My journey, with all its highs and lows, would have been incomplete without the unwavering support and dedication of my wife, Mrs. Krishna Kumari Sharma. Born on 26th September, 1951, in Budh Nagar Khandwa, Taluk Chandausi of Moradabad district in Uttar Pradesh, she has been a constant pillar of strength. Managing her responsibilities with grace and resilience, she embodies dedication and perseverance.

Education and Profession

Krishna's educational journey was marked by excellence. She completed her Bachelor of Science (BSc) from Maitreyi College, University of Delhi, in 1971. Following this, she pursued a Bachelor's and Master's in Education (B.Ed. and M.Ed) from Jamia Millia Islamia University, Delhi. Her career began as a lecturer at a B.Ed. College in Meerut, where she shared her knowledge and nurtured future educators.

Plate 62
One year old 'Baby Krishna', clicked by her father with a camera he brought from Japan in 1952.

Plate 63
Miss Krishna Kumari Sharma (1970, New Delhi): A portrait of wisdom, grace and unwavering strength.

Her passion for teaching extended beyond the classroom, as she volunteered to provide free tuition to underprivileged children even after our marriage. Her commitment to education and her generosity in offering free lessons exemplified her selflessness and belief in the power of knowledge.

Due to her mother's apprehensions about her travel and stay in Meerut, Krishna decided to explore the fields of marketing and management. She earned a Diploma in Business Administration from Bhartiya Vidya Bhawan and subsequently secured a position as a Marketing Assistant at Engineering Projects India Limited (EPI), a government enterprise under the Ministry of Heavy Industries. Working in Connaught Place, one of Delhi's most prestigious commercial hubs, she earned a respectable salary, a significant achievement at the time and a testament to her hard work and capabilities.

A Lady of Strength and Resilience: A Partner in True Sense

Krishna has demonstrated an extraordinary ability to adapt to different situations. Shortly after our marriage, she left her lucrative job and accompanied me to Germany, adjusting to life there despite the brief stay. We later moved to Nigeria, where we spent over ten years, a vastly different experience compared to Germany.

Her strength and endurance were evident when she gave birth to our first child, our eldest daughter, in Nigeria, far from our relatives. Managing everything with minimal support, she relied on letters, which took 20-25 days to reach and sometimes never arrived. Through these letters, she communicated with family, sought

Plate 64
Myself with my wife Krishna, one of the favourite pictures of our children, as they say; 1978, Jaipur, Rajasthan.

advice on traditions, and endeavoured to carry forward our customs and celebrations even while living abroad.

When we decided to return to India and settle down, Krishna readily supported my decision and very comfortably left the luxurious life abroad. She adapted seamlessly to life in a traditional joint family with my parents, younger brother and his wife in Jaipur, and took exceptional care of my ageing parents.

In 1995, we built a house within our family compound to provide better facilities for our children's education. While I could visit Jaipur only on weekends from Fatehpur Shekhawati, Krishna shouldered the responsibility of overseeing the construction. Throughout our marriage, what truly set her apart was her unwavering support for me and our family.

> *"A successful marriage is an edifice that must be rebuilt every day."*
>
> *- Andre Maurois*

A Nurturing Mother

Krishna's role as a mother has been nothing short of remarkable. During my assignments in Fatehpur and Bikaner, she single-handedly managed our home and children, allowing me to focus on my work without concern. Her efficient management ensured our home ran smoothly and our children were well cared for. Her influence on our children's education and upbringing has been profound. She instilled in them the values of hard work, discipline, and kindness. Our elder daughter's academic excellence, our son's dedication, as well as our younger daughter's career success, are all testaments to Krishna's constant encouragement and guidance.

Her contribution to our family extends beyond her maternal role. Her presence has always been a source of warmth and comfort. She has been my confidante, advisor and rock. Her wisdom and patience have guided me through many challenging times, and her love and care have been the bedrock of our family.

Family Legacy

Krishna's traits are a reflection of her parents. My father-in-law, Shri Ram Swaroopji Sharma, was influential yet humble and pleasant. My mother-in-law, Smt. Ganga Devi Sharma, was simple, motherly and affectionate. She is the eldest of the five siblings, including her sister, Kusum, and three brothers, Rakesh, Rajesh, and Ravi.

My Father-in-Law: A Pillar of Simplicity and Influence:

My father-in-law was a man of remarkable contrasts, both simple and influential. His influence was evident in how swiftly he could get things done, a testament to his character and reputation. He came from a family of five brothers, with him being the eldest. Unlike his siblings who stayed back in the village to manage their agricultural lands, my father-in-law ventured to Delhi for a career in service.

He rose from humble beginnings to become the Private Secretary to the Cabinet Secretary, Government of India and Under Secretary, General Administration at Rashtrapati Bhavan (President House). After his retirement in 1982, he was offered by the Governor of West Bengal, Mr B.D. Pandey to join him as his personal secretary at the 'Raj Bhavan' (The Governor House). This was a testament to his capability and trustworthiness.

Plate 65
My father in law, Shri Ram Swaroopji Sharma, a man of influence yet simplicity, with my mother in law, Smt Ganga Devi Sharma, a figure of affection.

Plate 66 - *My wife Krishna with her siblings, Mr Rakesh, Mr Rajesh, Mrs Kusum and sisters in law, Mrs Sunita and Mrs Meenakshi, on the occasion of Rakshabandhan, 22nd August, 2021, New Delhi*

From the Raj Bhavan, he wrote to us about the facilities he was given there, all reflecting the high regard in which he was held. However, after some time in Calcutta, due to some family circumstances, he had to come back to Delhi. He passed away in 1984 by a massive heart attack.

Throughout these experiences, my father-in-law remained a figure of strength and resilience. His letters, filled with wisdom and warmth, are treasured memories of his enduring love and dedication.

The Tragic Fate

In 1988, tragedy struck our family once more. Just as we returned to India from Nigeria in September, we were looking forward to attend my youngest brother-in-law Ravi's wedding, as we had already missed Rakesh, Rajesh and Kusum's marriage while being abroad. However, fate had other plans. On 1st December of the same year, our beloved Ravi met with a fatal road accident. The loss was devastating and left an enduring void in our lives.

Today, my two brothers-in-law are settled in Delhi, while my sister-in-law and her family have recently moved to Faridabad.

> *"Behind every great man, there's a woman giving strength and comfort, in the background of which one thrives."*

As I look back on our journey together, I realise that Krishna's role has been pivotal in shaping our family's story. Her sacrifices, dedication, and unwavering support have been the foundation upon which we have built our lives. She has been more than just a wife; she has been a partner in every sense, sharing in all the joys and sorrows, successes and failures.

In essence, she is the heart and soul of our family. Her contributions, often made quietly and without fanfare, have been immeasurable. She has been the guiding light, the silent strength, and the unwavering support that has held our family together. Her legacy of love, dedication, and selflessness will continue to inspire us all.

Plate 67
Our 40th Marriage anniversary, 1st June, 2017, Jaipur.
Celebrating four decades of love. togetherness and countless memories.

Chapter 12

Sowing New Beginnings: Defying Stereotypes in Agriculture

In September 1988, after a decade of residing and working in Nigeria, I made the monumental decision to relocate my family back to India. My tenure as a faculty member at the university in Nigeria had been fulfilling, but it was time to prioritise my parents, my extended family, and the future of my children.

I approached the university administration with my request not to renew my contract. They were understanding and even asked me to recommend a competent replacement for my position, demonstrating their appreciation for my work.

Back in India, however, I had no job lined up. The transition was daunting, but I was resolute. I informed my colleagues in Nigeria of my plan to return to India and purchase agricultural land to start farming. The reactions were mixed. Some supported the idea, recognizing the value of my expertise, while others were sceptical, questioning the respectability and financial viability of farming as a profession.

One colleague from Udaipur, with an agricultural background, expressed his doubts directly. "Sharmaji, are you really going to do farming?" he asked. I affirmed my decision, explaining that professionals in other fields, such as medicine and engineering, often returned to India to start their own practices or businesses without facing judgement. Why should my return to agriculture be viewed any differently?

The perception in India at that time was that agriculture was neither a lucrative nor a respectable profession. It was seen as a fallback rather than a career of choice, and I was determined to challenge this misconception. I stood firm, driven by a passion for agriculture and a belief in its importance.

I wanted to prove that farming could be a dignified and rewarding career. My decision was not just about making a living but about making a statement. I aimed to show that with knowledge, dedication, and modern techniques, farming could be both respectable and profitable.

Upon returning to India, I began the process of searching for land and setting up my farming operations. It was a challenging transition. There were numerous logistical hurdles to overcome, from securing the right land to learning the specifics of local agricultural practices.

Yet, I approached these challenges with the same vigour and determination that had guided my academic career. My approach was not just about farming but about leveraging my academic background and expertise to introduce scientific methods to agriculture.

Understanding the importance of expert advice, I reached out to professionals and experts from the Agricultural Department of the Rajasthan Government. I planned to collaborate with them to ensure my farming practices were rooted in the latest research and innovations. Additionally, having studied at IARI in Delhi, I intended to seek guidance and support from the Agricultural Faculty and researchers there. My goal was not only to pursue farming successfully but also to inspire the local farming community to adopt scientific methods through Extension Services.

Despite my clear vision and strategic approach, many people couldn't see beyond their traditional perceptions. They judged me, thinking I would be manually ploughing the fields. What they failed to understand was that my strategy was much more sophisticated and future-oriented. I envisioned pioneering efforts in seed production, aiming to bring high-value vegetable seeds to Rajasthan, supported by collaborations with agricultural experts and scientific communities in Delhi and beyond. I had already scouted land about 40 kilometres from Jaipur.

In the 1980s, the agricultural sector in India was still developing, and the application of science and technology was limited. Many of the concepts and methods I considered progressive then are still not widely adopted by the majority of farmers today. My vision was ahead of its time, aiming to revolutionise local farming practices and increase productivity and profitability through scientific methods.

Despite my determination and efforts, challenges were increasing. There was a lack of collaboration between the private and public sectors, a lack of awareness among locals, and negligible support from organisations, both in terms of finances and manpower.

Today, I see the importance of organic farming, environmental sciences, and forest development projects, all of which have become crucial. I realise now how my thinking and vision were ahead of their time.

Amidst these challenges, destiny led me to secure a temporary but respectable job with the Council of Scientific and Industrial Research (CSIR), established during Prime Minister Pandit Nehru's tenure.

In 1958, amid the brain drain phenomenon, CSIR was conceived to retain talent within India by offering prestigious roles equivalent to class-one officers. It aimed to provide fulfilling positions to prevent frustration among those returning from abroad and later expanded to include Indian scientists with higher degrees from within India too.

I was appointed as part of the scientist pool, a position that marked the beginning of a significant phase in my career. I joined as a Scientist Pool Officer at the Agricultural Research Station (ARS), Durgapura, Jaipur. This role provided me with the platform to apply my knowledge and skills in a meaningful way. The scientist pool was a unique initiative aimed at integrating returning scholars and researchers into India's developmental framework, ensuring they could contribute effectively to the nation's progress.

> *"In every seed planted lies the hope for a sustainable future; a future where family, community, and the land thrive together."*

Chapter 13

A Transformative Tenure at the Agricultural Research Station, Fatehpur-Shekhawati

As time passed, my career journey led me to significant opportunities in field research. In 1989, I was appointed as an Associate Professor at the Agricultural Research Station (ARS) in Fatehpur-Shekhawati, a city renowned for its historic 'Havelis'. Its rich history and stunning architecture make it a prominent tourist destination.

Having accumulated ten years of teaching experience in both undergraduate and postgraduate programs in Nigeria, I sought a similar position of a teaching faculty at Rajasthan Agricultural University (RAU). However, no openings were available at that time. Consequently, I joined ARS Fatehpur, which was also a part of RAU. The campus, located in a forested area away from the city, was environmentally clean and serene.

This research station was dedicated to advancing agricultural practices and innovations, a field that had always been close to my heart. Moving to ARS Fatehpur marked a pivotal shift in my career, allowing me to delve deeper into agricultural research and make meaningful contributions to the local farming community.

The Day of Joining:

My first day at ARS Fatehpur, 20th November, 1989, is memorable for two reasons. Firstly, I was unfamiliar with the route to Fatehpur-Shekhawati. Secondly, it was the day of the general elections for the Lok Sabha in India, and most of the staff was on election duty.

My father was particularly concerned about whether I would manage to join, given that I had requested an extension for personal reasons earlier. To my relief, I successfully navigated my way to ARS Fatehpur, located on National Highway 11. Upon arrival, I found minimal staff present, with the officer in charge being Dr. Abhey Singh Rathore. It turned out that Dr. Rathore and I were from the same BSc Agriculture batch, though from different colleges, myself from Udaipur and he from Jobner.

After completing the official joining formalities and enjoying a cup of tea, he informed me that there was little to be done for the day, and I could return to Jaipur. I boarded a bus to Jaipur from a temporary bus stop outside the campus. When my father saw me back around 2:30 pm, he wondered whether I could join or not, but was relieved and pleased to hear about my successful joining.

Family Arrangements:

During this period, I left my wife and children with my parents in Jaipur. Although it was a difficult decision, it was necessary for the stability and well-being of my family. It was important for my children to experience life in a joint family, especially with my parents.

This experience is fondly remembered by my elder daughter. The decision was deeply rooted in my own experiences; having never met my grandparents, I wanted my children to enjoy this privilege. Additionally, as my father had always emphasised the importance of education, I wanted the same for my children and thus decided to continue their schooling in Jaipur.

I lived alone at my workplace, managing my cooking and daily needs independently. This arrangement continued for thirteen years, a significant portion of my professional life. Although living apart from my family was challenging, it taught me resilience and self-reliance.

Life in Fatehpur:

The campus was situated about seven kilometres from the main township of Fatehpur-Shekhawati, on the route from Jaipur. The distance from the city hustle and the sprawling fields added to its charm and tranquillity.

The campus was beautifully planned, featuring spacious family quarters, a playground, an office building, a cooperative grocery shop, a guest house, and extensive agricultural fields. My allocated house was a three-bedroom property with a front lawn and a backyard. The weather ranged from extreme cold to scorching heat, often reaching 50 degrees Celsius. Several

Plate 68
Senior Scientists at Agricultural Research Station (ARS), Fatehpur Shekhawati, Rajasthan. Clicked during a casual get together in the evening.

scientists, including married bachelors, commuted weekly to Jaipur, which was 145 kilometres away.

Daily life included tea with friends after office hours in a Round-Robin manner. After dinner at 9 PM, we often took a walk to the guest house, which boasted a lush green garden. Some friends would relax on the grass, enjoying the cool breeze late into the night, especially during summer.

Sharing not only professional life, but also moments of joys and struggle, discussions about the families left at native places and concerns of growing children, all this strengthened the bond of friendship among the colleagues there. I still stay in touch with a few of them, namely Dr. A.S.Rathore, Dr.J.P.Verma, Dr.D.K.Saxena, Dr.R.B.L.Gupta, Dr.P.S. Shekhawat and Dr.G.L.Keshwa. Although now the conversations centre around settled children, grandchildren, challenging health issues with age, pension processing etc.

The Morning Walk Routine

A significant routine of my life, the morning walk, began in 1996 with Dr.J.P.Vermaji, who was my immediate neighbour. This habit continued for the next 28 years till my health permitted me. It was a routine which I followed in all seasons and circumstances, irrespective of the further change of cities or seasons, be it monsoon pouring, chilling mornings or scorching summers. It instilled and fostered in me a lot of mental strength, endurance, discipline and most importantly physical fitness, which paid a lot in the journey ahead. Most of the time alone, but sometimes with changing companions, whoever liked to join; friends, neighbours, my children, son in law, and later even my grandchildren, but the walk continued.

The Awaited Summer Vacations

During summer vacations, while many colleagues sent their families away, I welcomed mine to Fatehpur. My children eagerly anticipated these vacations, relishing the countryside's rustic charm. Early in the morning, I used to take them to the fields. They enjoyed exploring the fields, playing in cool waters, and experiencing the sunrise from sand dunes. Standing on top of the dunes and watching a train pass by, through the fields used to be a moment of joy for them. Despite the heat, the early mornings and evenings were pleasant. We would often sleep in the backyard at night, enjoying the cooler temperatures.

While some colleagues questioned why I brought my family during the sweltering summer, my children cherished the experience. They developed friendship with the children still remaining in the campus during the summer vacations, and used to get involved in playing table tennis, carrom and cards, mostly in the evenings. They would spend their days exploring the area, cycling through the scenic routes, and indulging in comic books. The joy and freedom they experienced was evident on their faces. On the whole, it was a memorable and enjoyable experience for my family, leaving lasting memories.

My Role at ARS: Demanding Yet Fulfilling

My role at the Agricultural Research Station (ARS) was both demanding and fulfilling. I was deeply involved in projects aimed at enhancing crop yields, developing

Plate 69
My children enjoying morning visit to the fields. Standing on the dunes and watching the train pass by were moments of joy for them (1992).

Plate 70
My family at our initial residence in ARS Fatehpur Shekhawati, during the summer vacations of children (1992).

sustainable farming practices, and introducing innovative techniques to local farmers.

We held biannual meetings, one for the Kharif season and another for the Rabi season. These meetings, attended by the government agriculture department and progressive farmers, addressed various challenges faced by local farmers. We would either offer them suggestions and solutions, or would work on them. These solutions were often a result of field experiments conducted over years.

Weekly Visits to Jaipur: My Lifeline

Regardless of the season, whether it was the intense heat of summer or the biting cold of winter, I made a weekly journey between Jaipur and Fatehpur Shekhawati. Every week, I travelled home to spend weekends with my family. This routine became an integral part of my life during the thirteen years I spent at ARS Fatehpur. Though demanding, I embraced it wholeheartedly, valuing the time spent at home. These trips were more than just routine; they were a lifeline that connected me to my loved ones.

Our home in Jaipur, while lacking some luxuries we enjoyed in Nigeria, was still well-equipped compared to others in our neighbourhood. We were one of the few families with a landline telephone and a television, which was a luxury at that time.

Our house became a hub for the neighbourhood, where people gathered to make phone calls or watch popular TV shows like *Mahabharata* and *Ramayana*. '*Doordarshan,*' the only TV channel available then, brought families, friends, and neighbours together, sharing stories and laughter. My elder daughter still fondly remembers those serials as a significant part of her childhood.

Parental Devotion and Support

I have always been deeply attached to my children, a trait I believe I inherited from my father. He was meticulous about accompanying me wherever I went, whether to Udaipur, New Delhi, or seeing me off for my travels abroad. This level of involvement left a profound impact on me and instilled in me a sense of responsibility and care.

Similarly, I have been actively involved in my children's academic journeys. Whenever their board exams approached, I would take leave from work to support them. Whether it was their board exams or crucial entrance exams like the IIT JEE, I made it a point to be present at their examination centres.

My colleagues in Fatehpur-Shekhawati often questioned why I took leave for my grown-up children, but their opinions never swayed me. I wanted to support them in every way possible.

In 1996, when my daughter Sangita had her 12th board exams and my son Ankur had his 10th board exams, both had a common exam centre. I would take Sangita for her morning exams, wait for three hours, then bring her back home around noon. In the afternoon, I would take Ankur for his exams, wait another two and a half hours, and then return home. I was always glad to be there for them.

I also accompanied my children to their college entrance exams, counselling sessions, and college admissions. I travelled with them to JLN Medical College in Ajmer, coaching centres in Kota and IITs in Bombay and Varanasi. This consistent support provided them with a sense of security and motivation during these crucial times.

In essence, just as my father had been there for me, I made sure to be there for my children, offering unwavering support and encouragement throughout their educational journeys. I knew that my presence and encouragement were invaluable to their success.

> *"Balancing tradition with modernity,*
> *we sow the seeds for a brighter future."*

Reflections on the Journey

Shekhawati, with its expansive fields and the hum of agricultural research, profoundly shaped my perspective. It taught me resilience amidst change, an appreciation for simplicity, and the enduring value of family bonds. Each chapter of this journey, from Jaipur to Shekhawati, resonates with lessons learned and memories cherished—a journey that continues to inspire and define my life's path.

Plate 71
Myself with my Elder son in law, Dr Vaibhav Vaishnav and my grandson, Arjun, at ARS, Fatehpur Shekhawati, during a casual visit in June, 2017.

Chapter 14

A Brief and Impactful Stint at the Directorate of Research

After spending thirteen years in Fatehpur, my transfer to the Directorate of Research at University Headquarters in Bikaner in November 2002 marked a significant change, blending nostalgia with anticipation for new beginnings.

Throughout my tenure, I pursued opportunities in teaching, a passion that continually fuelled my aspirations. Unfortunately, I was unable to secure a teaching position and continued in research-oriented roles, which had also been close to my heart.

Finally, I found myself at the doorstep of the Directorate of Research, a pivotal figure whose purview spanned the entire university. This opportunity provided me with experience of wider research administration. My responsibilities included coordinating a network of nine agricultural research stations across Rajasthan, akin to the diverse challenges and opportunities that Fatehpur had once presented.

The role demanded meticulous compilation of data, aligning with the rhythm of two distinct cropping seasons every six months. Over the next four and a half years, I immersed myself in advancing agricultural research, overseeing research output across various stations and reviewing numerous projects for their relevance and impact. During my Bikaner stay, I used to visit Jaipur once in a fortnight.

A Moment of Pride: Book Launch by Honourable Mrs. Pratibha Patil.

One of the highlights of my career occurred on 23rd March, 2006, during the convocation of the Rajasthan Agricultural University (RAU) in Bikaner. The Chief Guest, Mrs. Pratibha Patil, the then Governor of Rajasthan and Chancellor of the University, graced the event.

Besides awarding degrees, Mrs. Patil launched our book, "*Faslon ki Unnat Kismein*" (Improved Varieties of Crops), a compilation co-authored with Dr. D.K. Garg. I cherish the copy of the book signed by the Honourable Governor, a moment captured in a photograph later framed and presented to me by the Directorate staff.

In the very next year, 2007, the year of my retirement too, Mrs. Patil was sworn in as India's 12th President, becoming the first woman to hold the position.

The Young Companions: Bond of Respect and Affection

After thirteen years of cooking for myself in Fatehpur, I decided to forgo routine cooking for the last four and a half years before retirement. I knew that dining out wasn't ideal in the long-term. I was fortunate enough that I landed in a rented room, having three BHK setup. The other occupants were veterinary college students,

Plate 72 - 23rd March, 2006, the convocation of the Rajasthan Agricultural University, Bikaner. Honourable Mrs. Pratibha Patil, the then Governor of Rajasthan and Chancellor of the University launched our book, "Faslon ki Unnat Kismein" (Improved Varieties of Crops), a compilation I co-authored with Dr. D.K. Garg.

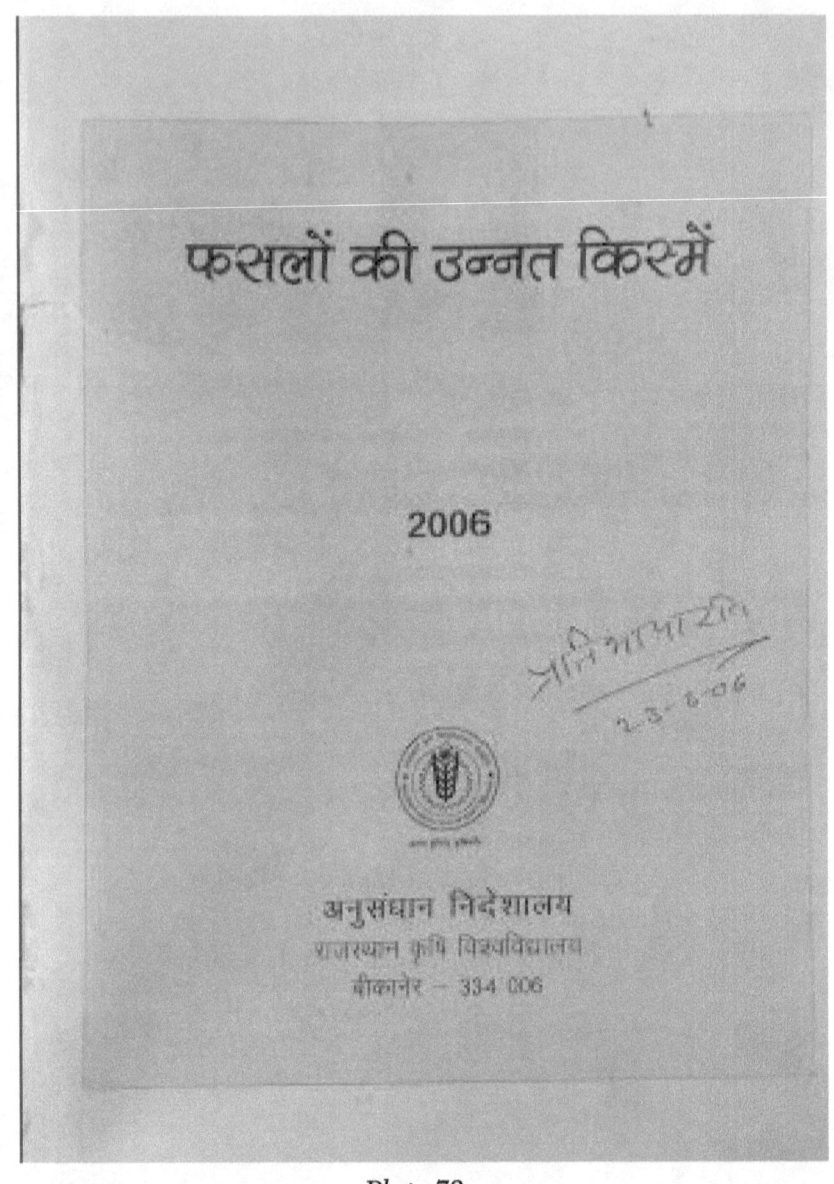

Plate 73
A copy of our book "Faslon ki Unnat Kismein" launched and signed by the Honourable Governor of Rajasthan, Mrs Pratibha Patil.

a part of our university. They were very sincere and respectful to me, and offered to start a mess with a cook. I readily accepted as it was a nice option of getting home cooked food. This arrangement continued even after the first batch of students graduated and were replaced by their juniors.

The initial residents were Dr. Prithvi Singh and Dr. Vishal Singh, both from Rajasthan. After graduation, Dr. Prithvi pursued a postgraduate course in Food and Agri Business Management at IIM Ahmedabad and later launched his own startup.

Dr. Vishal Singh joined the Veterinary Department in the Punjab government. Later, Dr. Aman Rustagi joined us in the 3BHK setup. Upon completion of his graduation, Aman served in the Veterinary Core of the Indian Army initially, and currently is a Commandant in the Home Guards Department of Rajasthan. I am still in contact with them and whenever they happen to be in Jaipur, they make sure to visit me.

Hanging Up the Boots: My Retirement Day

On 30th March, 2007 (as 31st was a holiday), following 18 years of service, my retirement day arrived. It was a mix of satisfaction, accomplishment and relief, coupled with excitement to reunite with my family. This was a reunion with my mother, wife, children, and extended family.

When we returned from Nigeria in 1988, my elder daughter was 9 years old, and by my retirement, she was already married in July 2006. Despite my weekly and

Plate 74
30th March, 2007, the day of my retirement at the Directorate of Research, Bikaner, following 18 years of service at the Rajasthan Agricultural University.

Plate 75
With Dr M.P.Sahu, the Director Research, on my Retirement Day.

Plate 76
Colleagues and staff bidding farewell on my retirement. My wife, daughters and elder son in law also joined.

Plate 77
Returning to my hometown and embracing my mother after retirement: a moment of pure joy.

later fortnightly visits from Fatehpur and Bikaner, I felt a deep sense of having missed out on watching my children grow up.

The farewell party at the Directorate of Research was emotional, with colleagues and the Director, Dr. M.P. Sahu, offering heartfelt words of appreciation.

I still remember the morning, the last day in my chamber, on my seat. The final day in my office was marked by traditional customs; my turban tied (Bandhej Safa), the sentimental speeches, the garlands, the pictures clicked, my farewell speech and finally the convoy of cars and jeeps escorting me and my family to the campus guest house where I had recently shifted. My wife, elder daughter with her husband, and younger daughter joined the celebration, though my son could not attend due to his MBA exams in Bangalore.

The following day, I hosted a farewell party for my Directorate colleagues and staff from related departments such as Seed Testing, Agriculture College, Agricultural Research Station at Bikaner and the Registrar's Office to express my gratitude for the association, although for a small period but a significant one.

My family also visited notable places in Bikaner, including the Karni Mata Temple, renowned as the 'Rat Temple', situated in a town called Deshnok, around 30 kms from Bikaner. It was really a wonder to see rats all around the temple premises. We also visited the Lalgarh Palace, famous for its architectural brilliance and amalgamation of Indian, European and Mughal architecture. We still have the pictures clicked by my son in law in the lush lawns and with the heritage art pieces of the museum there. These were moments of joy and contentment.

During our journey back to Jaipur, we had a stopover at the Agricultural Research Station (ARS), Fatehpur Shekhawati. As I had spent a major part of my service years in Fatehpur, our colleagues were kind enough to organise a small farewell party there too, reliving old memories.

Upon reaching Jaipur, I received a warm and eagerly awaited welcome from my mother, siblings, and the extended family. Despite the happiness of the reunion, I carried a deep sorrow in my heart. During this period I had lost my respected father in December 2000.

Reflecting on a Rich and Fulfilling Journey

Now that I have retired for quite some time, I am living with my family completely contended, cherishing the experiences, the memories, the strength, the beautiful relationships and bonds I have accumulated. My professional life, through its various phases, was always supported by my family's strength and encouragement.

Reflecting on these years, I recognize that the challenges and transitions were part of a larger journey, shaping our lives. Each phase, whether in Germany, Nigeria or India, contributed to the rich tapestry of our experiences. The lessons learned, resilience developed and bonds strengthened have been pivotal in defining who we are today.

Chapter 15

The Circle of Belonging:
The Tree of Modern Joint Family

My family's origin can be traced to a small village near Jaipur. My father, Shri Mangi Lalji Sharma, son of Shri Shiv Shankarji Sharma, was born on 15th August, 1910, in the village of Udaipuria. His life stands as a testament to resilience, social reform, and unwavering integrity. It is quite easy to remember his birth date, coinciding with India's Independence Day many years later.

He had a significant turning point in his early life when, at the age of 10, he was adopted by his uncle in Jaipur. This adoption brought a new chapter in his life, but it also came with its own set of challenges.

As my father approached his twenties, his adopted father passed away, leaving a void and triggering a series of events that tested his principles and fortitude. A traditional practice called 'Mrityu Bhoj' came into play. In this custom, the bereaved family, irrespective of their financial status, would host a feast for the Brahmins and invite the villagers. Often, this would lead families to incur debts. My father, a social reformer at heart, did not believe in this practice. This led to a conflict with his adopted mother, who insisted on following the tradition.

The disagreement escalated to a court case. Initially, my father won in the lower court, thanks to witnesses who testified that he was indeed adopted. However, the high court ruled against him due to a lack of documentary evidence of adoption. As a result, he had to leave his home and his mother, moving forward on his own. By 1932, he got married, and in 1935, my eldest sister was born.

Their life wasn't easy. They left behind their ancestral home and all its wealth, including substantial amounts of money and jewellery, to live a modest life in a rented house. My father's decision to abandon all material possessions for the sake of his principles reflects his selflessness and honesty. He was a man of simplicity, integrity and unwavering honesty, qualities that shaped his interactions and decisions in every aspect of his life. Even though life presented him with numerous challenges, he faced them patiently with a calm resolve and an optimistic outlook.

In 1948, my father's life took another joyous turn with my birth on the 5th of October. The family continued to live modestly but with dignity and pride. Somehow, my official documents list my birth date as 10th March, 1947. This discrepancy in dates has always been a part of my story. By the time I was one and a half years old, my eldest sister got married in 1949, marking another significant event in our family history.

Family History

My mother, Smt. Champa Devi Sharma, hailed from an affluent family in Sarola, Maharashtra. She often reminisced about her childhood, recounting tales of golden bricks, a symbol of the wealth and prosperity her family enjoyed. Her grandfather was exceptionally wealthy, maintaining a large household staff. She recalled how gunmen used to guard their house at night. She had the privilege of studying up to 5th grade, which was quite an achievement for that era. Marriages happened early in those days; my mother was only 13, and my father was 22 when they got married. This significant age difference was typical for that time.

My father, on the other hand, had no land or property to his name. He raised us in a rented house, relying solely on his own efforts. We were a large family, with three sisters and four brothers. Despite our modest means, my father ensured that we all received a good education. Even after coming from such an affluent background, my mother adapted well to the challenging conditions of our family life with my father. Despite their young and tender age at the time of marriage, they managed to build a life together, overcoming numerous challenges.

One of the poignant aspects of my life is that I never had the chance to meet any of my grandparents. My mother's parents passed away when she was very young, still in Maharashtra. My father's parents, who had moved from the village to Jaipur, had also passed away before I could meet them. This absence left a void in my life, as I never experienced the love and wisdom that grandparents can provide.

Reflecting on this, I made it a priority to ensure that my children had the chance to experience the love of their grandparents. While I was posted in Fatehpur and later in Bikaner (a duration of around 18 years with my weekly visits to Jaipur), I left my wife and children with my parents in Jaipur so that they could enjoy the warmth and affection that I could never experience.

> *"A family's strength lies in its unity, built on the foundation of love, trust, and shared history."*
>
> *- Anonymous*

Educational Legacy and Father's Profession

My father, despite his humble beginnings, was an educated man. Education was considered a high standard and rigorous endeavour in that era. He completed his matriculation, which was a significant achievement for those times. He had a profound appreciation for English grammar, often referring to the renowned book "Wren & Martin" to guide us. He would teach and explain concepts from it, demonstrating a deep understanding of the subject. This level of dedication to education and the importance placed on learning was exceptional and transcended in the future generations of our family.

My father had a passion for bookbinding, a craft that became his profession. He never hired any helpers or assistants, preferring to do the work himself. This commitment to his craft meant that our entire family, including my mother, sisters, and brothers, would often assist him. His bookbinding shop was located in the main market of Jaipur, close to our rented house. This central location, near a prominent landmark, the Hawa Mahal, was convenient for both his business and our daily lives.

My father's work ethics and dedication were evident in the way he managed his shop. Despite the availability of modern conveniences, he preferred to work alone, meticulously binding books with care and precision. This shop, nestled in the heart of Jaipur, became a hub of activity for our family. Many times, especially during exams, when our house lacked proper lighting, we would go to the shop to study under the better illumination there.

This environment fostered a sense of resilience and resourcefulness in us. We learned to value hard work, education, and the importance of family support. My father's passion for bookbinding not only provided for us but also taught us invaluable lessons about dedication and self-reliance.

A Journey of Loss and Resilience

On 28th December, 2000, a profound emotional upheaval shook me to the core. It was a time when I felt utterly orphaned, grappling with a sense of profound loss of my father. My mother, in her 80s, was at the heart of this turmoil. Her silent suffering from Alzheimer's disease became increasingly evident, marking a period of deep introspection and emotional turbulence for me.

Over the course of the next nine years from 2000 to 2009, I found myself gradually strengthening emotionally. The pivotal year was 2007, when I began exploring meditation (Vipassana) as a means to cope with the challenges life presented.

Amidst this journey of personal growth, another devastating blow struck in 2009 with the loss of my mother. This loss was so profound that it reshaped my understanding of life itself. The shock was intense, leaving an indelible mark on my soul.

Through these experiences, I learned to navigate the complexities of grief and resilience. Each challenge became a catalyst for personal growth, shaping me into the person I am today.

> *"True wealth is found not in possessions,
> but in the bonds of a loving family."*

Raised Together, Bound Forever: Introducing Siblings

My Eldest Sister: Smt Vidya Devi Sharma

My eldest sister, a remarkable woman, began her career as a teacher with a certificate in Hindi. Initially, this qualification was sufficient for securing a job in a school. However, a government mandate later required teachers to have completed their matriculation. This posed a significant challenge for her as she had no knowledge of English beyond the basic ABCs, although she was well-versed in Hindi and other subjects.

Despite these challenges, she displayed extraordinary determination. While managing her household and taking care of her four children, two sons and two daughters, living in a joint family and pursuing the school job, she continued her education. Her dedication was evident as she walked nearly a kilometre to fetch water, adhering to traditional customs by maintaining a veil in the colony, yet never wavering in her commitment to learning and self-improvement.

Plate 78
My parents, Shri Mangilalji Sharma and Smt Champa Devi Sharma, clicked on 26th January, 1971.

Family Photograph (Jaipur, 1989)

Top Row (From Left to Right) Mahesh Kumar Sharma (Eldest son), Trilok Raj Sharma (Second son), Kailash Chandra Sharma (Third son), Subhash Chandra Sharma (Youngest son)

Middle Row (From Left to Right) Shri Ravi Shankar Ji Sharma (Youngest son-in-law), Smt Champa Devi Sharma (Mother, Amma), Shri Mangi Lal Ji Sharma (Father, Kakaji), Shri Bhanwar Lal Ji Sharma (Eldest son-in-law), Shri Laxmi Narayan Ji Sharma (Second son-in-law)

Bottom Row (From Left to Right) Smt Shakuntala Sharma (Eldest daughter-in-law), Smt Krishna Kumari Sharma (Second daughter-in-law), Smt Shakuntala Sharma (Third daughter-in-law), Smt Vandana Sharma (Youngest daughter-in-law), Smt Aruna Sharma (Youngest daughter), Smt Sushila Sharma (Second daughter), Smt Vidya Devi Sharma (Eldest daughter)

Plate 79 – Our family ; My parents and we siblings, four brothers and three sisters, along with the spouses. Captured at our Jaipur residence, 1989.

(Note: The footnote shows the relations in reference to my parents).

Her eldest daughter accompanied her in the journey of higher education. Together, they graduated, but my sister did not stop there. She continued her academic pursuits, completing her Bachelor's degree in Education (B.Ed), followed by a Masters in Education (M.Ed). She later retired as a school principal. Her story is a testament to her incredible perseverance and the power of education to transform lives. She not only raised a family in traditional settings but also broke barriers, achieving significant milestones in her professional life.

The bond I share with her is of great respect and affection. After getting a job, in spite of her own family responsibilities, I remember how at times, she used to send money orders to me, while I was facing my own struggles during college days in Udaipur. She is a motherly figure for our family and holds a special place in my heart.

My brother-in-law Shri Bhanwar Lal Sharma also retired as a school principal. Unfortunately, he had a near fatal fall from which he could not recover and after a few years he passed away.

Second Sister: Smt. Sushila Devi Sharma

My second sister, who is about six years elder to me, was married in 1957. Her journey through life is intertwined with the story of her husband, my brother-in-law, Shri Laxmi Narayan Sharma, who became a significant figure in the world of journalism.

From the very beginning of his career, my brother-in-law joined 'Rajasthan Patrika', one of the most renowned daily newspapers in India. He started his journey with the newspaper as a General Manager and later retired as a partner.

My sister supported him through this journey, managing their home and family while he made strides in his career.

Elder Brother: Late Prof. Mahesh Kumar Sharma

My elder brother, Professor Mahesh Kumar Sharma, was a man of great intellect and dedication. He held double Masters (MA) in Political Science and Public Administration, showcasing his profound commitment to academia. His journey as an educator began in Raipur, which at the time was part of Madhya Pradesh before becoming a part of Chhattisgarh.

He joined the esteemed Ravishankar Shukla University, specifically the Chhattisgarh Post Graduate College, where he dedicated himself to teaching and mentoring students. His passion for education and his deep knowledge in his fields made him a respected figure in the academic community. After years of imparting knowledge and inspiring countless students, he retired as a professor in 2005. After 40 years of stay in Raipur he came back to Jaipur with his family. Though his elder daughter, our affectionate Alka, had already got married in Jaipur in 1991.

Beyond his role as an educator, my brother was also a prolific author. He wrote and published several books, contributing significantly to the body of knowledge in his disciplines.

Tragically, he passed away in 2012 due to a heart attack. His passing was a significant loss to our family and the academic community. Adding to the sorrow, his wife, Mrs Shakuntala Sharma (often called 'Badi Shakuntala' by elders in our family), who had been diagnosed with Parkinson's disease, also passed away in 2023.

My Immediate Younger Brother: Shri Kailash Chandra Sharma

My younger brother Shri Kailash Chandra Sharma remained in Government job throughout his service life. I think he was very lucky to remain in Jaipur and be with my parents while we all were away. As he remained with my father in Jaipur, he is the one who carries forward his legacy of community service and is active in the society events. He got married to Mrs Shakuntala Sharma (Chhoti Shakuntala) in February 1977, much before my marriage when I was still in Germany. He is a man of simplicity, known for his honesty and integrity in our community. Due to these traits, he has been unanimously elected as the treasurer of our Brahmin Society and has also held various significant positions in the national executive council.

My Youngest Brother: Prof. (Dr.) Subhash Chandra Sharma

My youngest brother Subhash, has always been close to my heart. My understanding with him right from our childhood has been amazing. He was with us in Nigeria also, with his wife Vandana, for two years when he joined the Ministry of Education, Maiduguri in June 1982. It is his greatness that he considers me as his mentor and role model though I think I am not worth it all. He is the most intelligent of all the siblings as far as academics is concerned. He holds an M.Com., M.A. Economics (with a Gold Medal), LLB and Ph.D. Apart from this, he has also done an eleven months course for Faculty Teachers at Indian Institute of Management at Ahmedabad (IIMA) and has been a commissioned officer in Air Wing (N.C.C.).

His adventurous spirit has inspired not just me but our entire family. While we've occasionally worried about the risks involved, his passion for adventure remains undeniable. For the past 48 years, he has been exploring every corner of India, often travelling by motorcycle or scooter along with his friend, Prof. B.K. Chourasia.

After retiring from the Ministry of Higher Education in Oman, he embarked on an 18-day trek with his elder son, Pranay, across the Great Himalayan Trail. This remarkable journey included destinations such as Mount Everest Base Camp, Kala Patthar, Renjo La Pass, Cho La Pass, Gokyo Lakes, and Gokyo Ri. He is currently settled in Jaipur.

Youngest Sister: Smt. Aruna Sharma

Next in line is my youngest sister, who also holds a graduation degree. She has been a steadfast presence in our lives, living close by, bringing joy and vibrancy to every festival and important family celebration.

My brother-in-law, Shri Ravi Shanker Sharma, dedicated his career to the Rajasthan Roadways service until his retirement. We recently had the pleasure of celebrating a significant milestone, the 50th anniversary of their marriage this year (2024). It was a joyous occasion for the entire family.

A Rare Blessed Brother

In my school days, there were free tuition classes, conducted in our vicinity in the evenings at a place known as 'The Study Circle'. I used to attend these classes, right from 1957. These classes were being conducted and managed by Shri B.L. Ajmeraji of the Commerce College,

Plate 80 - Diwali, 19th October, 2017, at our Jaipur residence; three generations of family together, including members from the USA, UAE, and across India. A cherished memory, marking our last Diwali with my son Ankur and nephew Gaurav

Plate 81
With my soul sister, Dr Sudha Jain (sitting in the centre)

University of Rajasthan. Shri Ajmeraji had three sons and a daughter.

Over time, a deep and affectionate brother-sister bond developed between his daughter and me. In 1964, when I was just 16 and left for Udaipur to continue my studies, I had no idea that this relationship, nurtured over the past seven years, would become a cherished part of my life. Every year on Rakshabandhan, just like my three sisters, she would also tie the sacred Rakhi on my wrist.

I still recall an incident that truly reflected her deep respect for me. At the time, she was the principal of a Government Music College in Jaipur. During a visit to her office, I was taken aback when she stood up from her seat, approached me, bowed down, and touched my feet in front of her staff, including a peon and a clerk. She then introduced me to them, saying, "He is my Bhaisahab." I was overwhelmed, deeply moved by her gesture. Although she is my soul sister, her love and respect make her no less dear to me than my three real sisters. May every brother be blessed with a sister like mine. Her name is Dr. (Mrs.) Sudha Jain.

Cherished Moments with My Grandchildren

Our elder daughter, Sangita and her family lived in an independent portion within our large joint family compound. This proximity allowed us to share countless moments together, filling our lives with laughter, joy, and a deep sense of connection. Her children, Prabhav (Ricky) and Arjun were particularly attached to me, creating a bond that brought immense happiness to my heart.

Plate 82a & 82b
With my grandsons (Sangita's sons), Prabhav (Ricky) and Arjun; nurturing the special bond across generations with joy and love.

While I couldn't teach them in the traditional sense, I found immense joy in sharing simple yet profound practices like Anapana, the initial stage of Vipassana meditation that focuses on breathing awareness. I would sit with them, explaining the process and using short 10-15 minute cassette recordings. These sessions became a cherished part of our routine, and the kids embraced them with enthusiasm. We even did exercises together, turning these moments into fun and engaging activities.

Every night, my grandchildren insisted on sleeping with me. "Hum Nana Ji ke paas hi soyenge," (We will sleep with Grandpa only) they would say with sparkling eyes. They would snuggle up in the basement, eagerly awaiting the bedtime stories I had promised. These stories were our special time together, a ritual that lasted until late at night, often around 11 or 11:30 PM. Initially, I told them various tales, but soon, I began sharing stories from Vipassana teachings, weaving lessons of morality and transformation into each narrative.

One of their favourites was the story of Angulimala, a notorious figure who sought to complete a garland of fingers by killing 1000 people. When he encountered Buddha after already killing 999, his life was transformed by Buddha's wisdom and compassion. Despite facing the villagers' wrath, Angulimala remained calm and kind, eventually attaining enlightenment. This story, among others, captivated the children, teaching them important lessons about non violence, compassion, patience, and inner peace.

Every night, before sleeping, I was ready to share another story. As I told each tale, I watched their faces light up with curiosity and excitement. After some time, however, I began to run out of new stories. When I started repeating them, the kids would quickly catch on, saying, "Nana Ji, we know this one already!" Their playful complaints were a testament to how much they enjoyed our storytelling sessions.

These moments with my grandchildren were incredibly precious. Watching them grow up, sharing stories, and imparting wisdom brought immense joy to my heart. Our time together was filled with laughter, learning, and love. I cherish every memory of those days, knowing that they are some of the best times of my life. The bond we created during those storytelling nights and shared activities is something I hold close to my heart, a treasure trove of beautiful moments that I will always remember.

The Evolution of Family Dynamics: Embracing the Modern Joint Family Life

In the bustling life of Jaipur, we embody the essence of a modern joint family setup. Four brothers and their families live together yet independently within a shared compound. The large plot features four separate houses, connected by a wide corridor that serves as a central hub for connection. This corridor is where we create joyful moments and share our stories, bridging our individual homes and fostering a close-knit family atmosphere.

After my retirement in 2007 from Bikaner, when I finally came to Jaipur to settle, a profound realisation struck me. My children had grown up significantly, and I had missed witnessing their entire childhood unfold. My elder daughter had got married after completing her post graduation in Obstetrics & Gynaecology, and my son and younger daughter were already employed. Reflecting on

Plate 83 - Featuring four brothers (including myself) and their wives, this photograph symbolizes the four pillars of our family, standing as a testament to our strength and unity.

this, I often find myself reminiscing about their childhood, a period I feel I have missed out on, amidst life's many responsibilities and challenges.

My father used to fondly remark, "**Just like birds fly in the morning, leaving their nests behind, but after pecking and having enough for the day, they come back to their nests (home) in the evening.**" This wisdom echoed through our daily lives, shaping our familial bonds and routines. My elder brother from Raipur, myself from Bikaner and my youngest brother from Oman, all returned to this place known as our home in Jaipur after retirement. Such was the vision of our father!

It's akin to a paradise, where happiness thrives in the company of family, especially now, during our retired years. This phase of life has been incredibly joyful for all of us, marked by togetherness and contentment.

Every day unfolds with a sense of belonging, fulfilment and strength, as we navigate through life's milestones and challenges together, We celebrate our unity and cherish the richness of our shared experiences, making this time of our lives truly special.

"The family is a safe haven where we are accepted, understood, and loved unconditionally."

- Anonymous

Chapter 16

Our Elder Daughter: The Pride of Our Family

Our elder daughter, Sangita, born on 23rd July, 1979, in Nigeria, has consistently been a beacon of excellence. Throughout her academic career, she has consistently achieved top ranks, often placing first or second in her class.

I once asked her out of curiosity if she had ever been third in her class. With a smile, she confidently replied, "First or second, never third." This response perfectly encapsulates her unwavering dedication and remarkable intelligence.

Reflecting on Sangita's journey fills me with immense pride and joy. Her academic and professional accomplishments are extraordinary, marking significant milestones in our family history.

Memories from Schooldays

I vividly remember returning to India from Nigeria in 1985 and going to collect Sangita's report card. I

Plate 84
Embracing Sangita, my firstborn, a moment of pure joy.

reviewed it carefully and noticed a discrepancy between the individual subject marks and the calculated total. Although the report card initially listed her as second in rank, I pointed out the error to her teacher. After a thorough review, the teacher acknowledged the mistake and issued a corrected report card, upgrading Sangita's rank to first.

Another memorable incident occurred when Sangita, while studying in India, mentioned that her teacher often used a wooden scale to punish students. As a university teacher myself, I strongly opposed physical punishment and advocated for counselling and positive reinforcement. Sangita was only in first grade at the time, so I decided to address the issue. The teacher surprisingly told me that Sangita says " My father has conveyed that I should not be hit'. She asked me, 'Sir did you say so?', and was astonished when I admitted. I respectfully questioned such practice and emphasised that corporal punishment was not appropriate for children. After a respectful conversation, the teacher acknowledged the validity of my concerns. Sangita still fondly recalls this incident with pride.

These experiences taught our children valuable lessons about advocating for fairness.

Her Journey Ahead

Sangita's study habits were unique and impressive. She often retreated to the rooftop to study, all while enjoying the distant sounds of film songs from a nearby marriage garden. Her ability to focus amidst distractions was evident during board examinations and the rigorous Pre-Medical Test (PMT). Her retention capacity was truly astounding and left us in awe.

> *"The journey of a thousand miles begins with one step."*
>
> *- Lao Tzu*

Throughout her MBBS, Sangita consistently excelled, earning gold medals for the highest marks in all three professional exams at the University of Rajasthan. Her achievements were particularly remarkable given that there was no prior medical background in our family. Her determination and hard work set a new standard for all of us and became a source of inspiration.

Beyond academics, Sangita demonstrated versatility, serving as the Head Prefect at her school and later as the Girls' Representative in the medical college students' union. She enjoys dancing and music and is an accomplished orator. She was the one who encouraged me to embark on writing this autobiography.

Today, she channels her brilliance and dedication into her role as the Director of Jaipur Fertility Centre, the oldest IVF centre in Jaipur, established in 1989 by Dr. M.L. Swarankar.

Her transition from a diligent student to a respected professional in the medical field is a testament to her perseverance and intellect. We are incredibly proud of her achievements and the compassionate care she provides to countless couples striving to fulfil their dream of parenthood.

Sangita began her medical journey at JLN Medical College, Ajmer, where she completed her MBBS. She excelled in her postgraduate studies in Gynaecology and Obstetrics at Lady Hardinge Medical College in Delhi.

Plate 85
Dr Sangita Sharma as Director, Jaipur Fertility Centre

Plate 86 - Sangita with her loving husband, Dr Vaibhav Vaishnav and their sons, Prabhav (Ricky) and Arjun (the elder and younger one, respectively)

On 2nd July, 2006, she married Dr. Vaibhav Vaishnav, her batchmate of MBBS days. He hails from Bijapur, a village in Pali district of Rajasthan, in the Jawai region famous for leopards. Dr. Vaibhav has established a distinguished career and currently serves as the Head of Critical Care Medicine at Manipal Hospital, Jaipur. His dedication, leadership and managerial skills were notably demonstrated during the Covid pandemic.

Their journey began in Ajmer, where their first son, Prabhav (Ricky), was born on 21st March, 2008. They then moved to Delhi for further professional pursuits. Sangita's commitment to excellence led her to specialise further in reproductive medicine (FNB) from Sir Ganga Ram Hospital in Delhi after securing an all India first rank in the entrance exam, while Dr. Vaibhav pursued a fellowship in critical care medicine from Fortis Hospital.

They welcomed their second son, Arjun, on 28th June, 2011, and later returned to Jaipur in 2012 to focus on family life and their growing children. Sangita also travelled to Germany for a short course on laparoscopic surgery.

> *"Education is not preparation for life;*
> *education is life itself."*
>
> *- John Dewey*

Her expertise and dedication in the field of IVF have earned her respect and recognition. Recently, she was awarded the 'Dr. APJ Abdul Kalam Inspiration Award 2024' at Bharat Mandapam, New Delhi, for being the 'Most Trusted IVF Specialist in North India' on June 29, 2024, the honours done by Member of Parliament and Bollywood Actress Smt. Hema Malini.

I am also delighted that she is a teaching faculty member for MCh students at Mahatma Gandhi Medical

College and keeps discussing about publishing research papers, a subject close to my heart.

Sangita's career and family life embody a balance of professional achievement and personal fulfilment, contributing significantly to the medical field and nurturing a loving family. Presently, they are settled in Jaipur.

Chapter 17

Our Son: An Inspiring Tale of Dedication and Grit

Our son, Ankur, born on 21st January, 1981, holds a special place in my heart. He demonstrated an extraordinary level of dedication and hard work throughout his academic journey. When he achieved an impressive 85% in his 10th board exams (Rajasthan Board), he was elated to surpass his sister's performance.

This accomplishment was a testament to his relentless effort and determination. His preparation for the IIT Entrance Examination, renowned for its complexity and level of difficulty, showcased his unwavering spirit.

At home, we had a basement where Ankur would spend most of his time, either studying or catching up on sleep. The basement became his sanctuary, a space for intense focus and perseverance. He would only come upstairs for meals, promptly returning to his studies as soon as he finished eating. A notable exception to this routine occurred during cricket matches. Ankur was an

Plate 87
My son Ankur's first day to school, 1st April, 1984, Maiduguri, Nigeria

Plate 88
34 years later, a similar moment: taking my granddaughter Anjali to school for the first time in India, after her return from Dubai (October 2018)

ardent admirer of Sachin Tendulkar. Whenever Sachin came to bat, we would call Ankur upstairs. The joy on his face as he watched his idol was palpable. Once Sachin was out, Ankur would return to his studies, albeit with a hint of disappointment.

This balance of dedication to his studies and moments of joy watching cricket epitomises his character. Although he may not have had the natural brilliance of his sister, his unwavering commitment and ability to find motivation in small pleasures carried him through. His story is one of perseverance and determination, a testament to his hard work.

In 2000, Ankur succeeded in one of the most challenging exams, the IIT JEE, and went on to complete his B.Tech from IT BHU (now IIT Varanasi) in 2004.

Ankur's professional journey began with Infosys in India, filled with hope and determination. His initial training in Pune and subsequent posting in Bangalore marked the start of a promising career in the IT industry. Driven by ambition and a quest for growth, he transitioned into business management, earning an MBA from the prestigious International School of Management Excellence (ISME) in Bangalore.

His career path led him through several esteemed banking institutions, starting with Mashreq Bank in Dubai in 2007. There, he made significant contributions and forged lasting professional relationships. His journey continued with Emirates National Bank of Dubai (ENBD) and later the Commercial Bank of Dubai (CBD).

Ankur's tenure spanned across multiple banks, each step marked by dedication and steady advancement. He later transitioned to the insurance sector, joining MetLife

Plate 89
Mr Ankur Sharma, our son at Commercial Bank of Dubai, UAE

American Insurance Company as a Senior Insurance Manager in June 2018.

During his time from 2007 to 2018, Ankur frequently visited India. On 29th January, 2012, he married Pooja Sharma in India, as a part of an arranged marriage.

> *"Strength grows in the moments when you think you can't go on but keep going anyway."*
>
> *- Anonymous*

Beyond his professional achievements, Ankur was a man of remarkable spirit and resilience. He found joy in marathon running, a passion that took him across continents, from Cape Town to Rome, Dubai, the USA, Oman, and Paris. Each race was not only a physical challenge but also a testament to his unwavering determination and zest for life.

Tragically, on 20th August, 2018, fate dealt a devastating blow with Ankur's untimely passing in an unfortunate accident. The loss of our beloved son left an indelible void in our lives, a pain that words cannot fully express.

Ankur's wife, Pooja Sharma, hails from a Parashar Brahmin family near Jaipur. Her family is deeply rooted in spiritual practices and community service. She stood by Ankur as a pillar of strength throughout their journey together. After his passing, Pooja returned to India, pursued further studies, and now manages the household with resilience and grace.

Ankur's memory lives on in our hearts, cherished for his affection, sincerity, dedication, the memorable times we shared and the love and warmth he brought into our lives. He was a son that everyone would pray for,

Plate 90
Ankur running Dubai Marathon, living his passion.

Plate 91
With Ankur after he just completed Dubai Marathon, 2014. The Burj Al Arab, world's only 7 Star hotel, can be seen in the background.

obedient and caring. Family members often compared him to 'Shravan Kumar,' a mythological character known for his obedience and devotion towards his parents. Ankur's absence is deeply felt, yet his legacy of determination and passion continues to inspire us.

My Life in Dubai with My Beloved Son: A Memorable Chapter

In 2010, Ankur invited my wife and me to Dubai for the first time. Full of enthusiasm, he took us to many of the city's attractions. A particularly memorable moment was our visit to the Burj Khalifa (formerly known as Burj Dubai). Opened to the public in January 2010, we were fortunate to visit in April of the same year. At 828 metres, the Burj Khalifa, with its elevator reaching the 124th floor, is the tallest building in the world. The experience was truly exhilarating.

After staying in Dubai for about 28 days, we travelled to Oman to visit my youngest brother, Dr. Subhash Chandra Sharma. Oman, with its coastal areas and hills, is a country of remarkable natural beauty.

We spent about two weeks there before returning to India by the end of May. Ankur often missed us and wished to spend more time together. He would visit India twice a year and arranged for our visits to Dubai frequently, providing us with three-month visas, the maximum allowed.

We visited Dubai in 2013-14, 2014-15, 2016-17, and finally in 2017-18, primarily during the pleasant weather of the year end. These visits included witnessing the Burj Khalifa fireworks, where thousands of people gathered to celebrate the New Year. On one of these visits, my elder

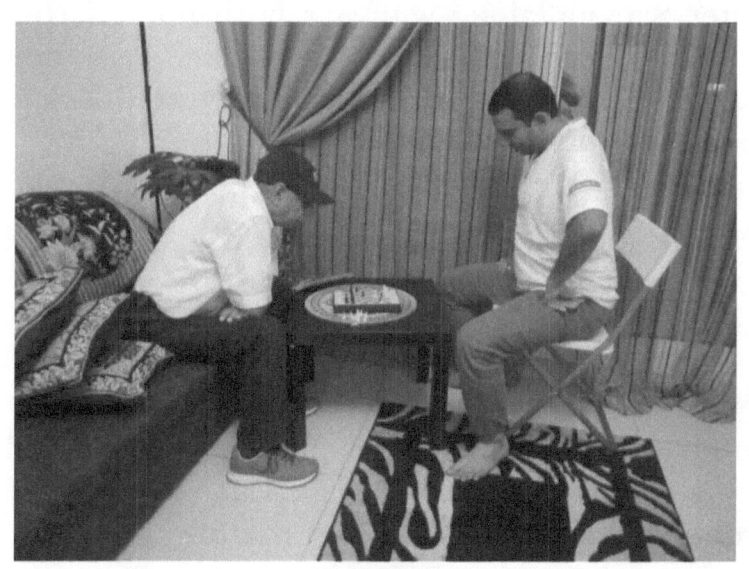

Plate 92
Playing Chess with Ankur at his residence in Dubai.

Plate 93
Having a cup of coffee at Sharjah Beach

daughter Sangita, along with her husband and children, joined us to see the fireworks. These were precious moments. My younger daughter also visited Ankur and Pooja in 2013 with her family.

Moreover, when Ankur planned his trips to the USA and Canada (2016) and South Africa (2018), he insisted that we accompany him. These trips became some of the most memorable moments of our lives.

Finding My Routine in a Foreign Land

In 1996, while living in Fatehpur, I developed a habit of morning walk. Fatehpur Shekhawati, with its serene environment, was ideal for this routine. I walked with colleagues and neighbours, and it became a daily ritual.

When I first visited Dubai in 2010, I sought out a place to continue my walking routine. Within a couple of days, I found an ideal spot with a kilometre-long green track near the Chambers of Commerce. It reminded me of the area around the Rashtrapati Bhavan in Delhi. I spent around 2-3 hours each day enjoying my walks.

Dubai felt like heaven to me. If asked about the best part of my life, I would always mention my time in Dubai. I was retired, free from any professional stress, and all three of my children were well settled. My practice of Vipassana meditation helped me remain calm and composed. The beautiful places for walks added to my joy.

My elder daughter visited Ankur and his family twice, once in 2015-16 and again in 2016-17. During her 2016-17 visit, my wife and I were already in Dubai. Being with family in a foreign land was special. Accommodation, food, and local transportation were convenient, thanks to Ankur's arrangements.

My time in Dubai was truly remarkable, offering stress-free living, physical activity, and quality time with my family. Each visit contributed to beautiful memories, making Dubai an unforgettable chapter in my life.

The Joy of Welcoming Our Granddaughter in Dubai: A Family Reunion

On 30th October, 2014, the arrival of my granddaughter, Anjali, brought immense joy to our family. This event made our Dubai memories even more special.

When Anjali was born, my younger brothers and their families joined us in Dubai to celebrate. It was a wonderful family reunion. My nephew Pranay, who works as the Head of Advanced Analytics Products at ENBD, was also there.

Every morning, my brothers and I would meet at what we fondly called the "Rashtrapati Bhavan." We would take long walks, sit and chat, and enjoy Indian samosas. These moments were incredibly special, strengthening our family bonds.

Plate 94 - Holding my bundle of joy with great pride; my granddaughter, Anjali

Plate 95 - Ankur with his wife Pooja and their newborn angel, Anjali (Guddu)

Plate 96 - Myself (in the centre) with my younger brothers, Mr Kailash (on left) and Dr Subhash (on right), enjoying morning walk at the lawns of Sharjah Chamber of Commerce and Industry, which we fondly used to compare with 'Rashtrapati Bhavan' in India. (2014)

Cherished Memories

The joy of spending time with Ankur, coupled with the beautiful surroundings, made this period one of the most cherished times of my life. Exploring the city together and enjoying simple pleasures created lasting memories.

In essence, Dubai holds a special place in my heart not only for its picturesque spots and relaxing atmosphere but also for the precious moments spent with my son. Attending Vipassana meditation courses there further enriched the experience. The arrival of my granddaughter and the time spent with family in such a beautiful city will always be treasured.

Plate 97
31st December, 2016, enjoying with Ankur and Sangita's family, while waiting for the spectacular new year's eve fireworks at Burj Khalifa.

Plate 98A - cherished family moment with loved ones in a foreign land; captured during Sangita's visit to Dubai, January 2017

Plate 99
With my son and elder daughter at Dubai Water Canal

Chapter 18

Our Younger Daughter:
A Story of Growth and Success

Our younger daughter, Er. Gunjan Sharma, embarked on her professional journey with a degree in Engineering (B.Tech.) from Jaipur Engineering College. Her career began at Trianz, a modest IT company in Bangalore.

This humble start marked the beginning of a promising career. With perseverance and hard work, she soon secured a position at Hewlett-Packard (HP), a renowned multinational IT company known for its hardware, software, and related services.

In 2009, Gunjan made a significant decision to leave her role at HP and return to Jaipur. On 17th April, 2009, she married Er. Sunil Sharma, who holds a degree in Computer Science and an MBA. Gunjan chose to prioritise family life at this point.

Despite the shift in focus and a brief teaching stint at an engineering college in Jaipur, along with roles at a few local IT companies, she remained steadfast. Her

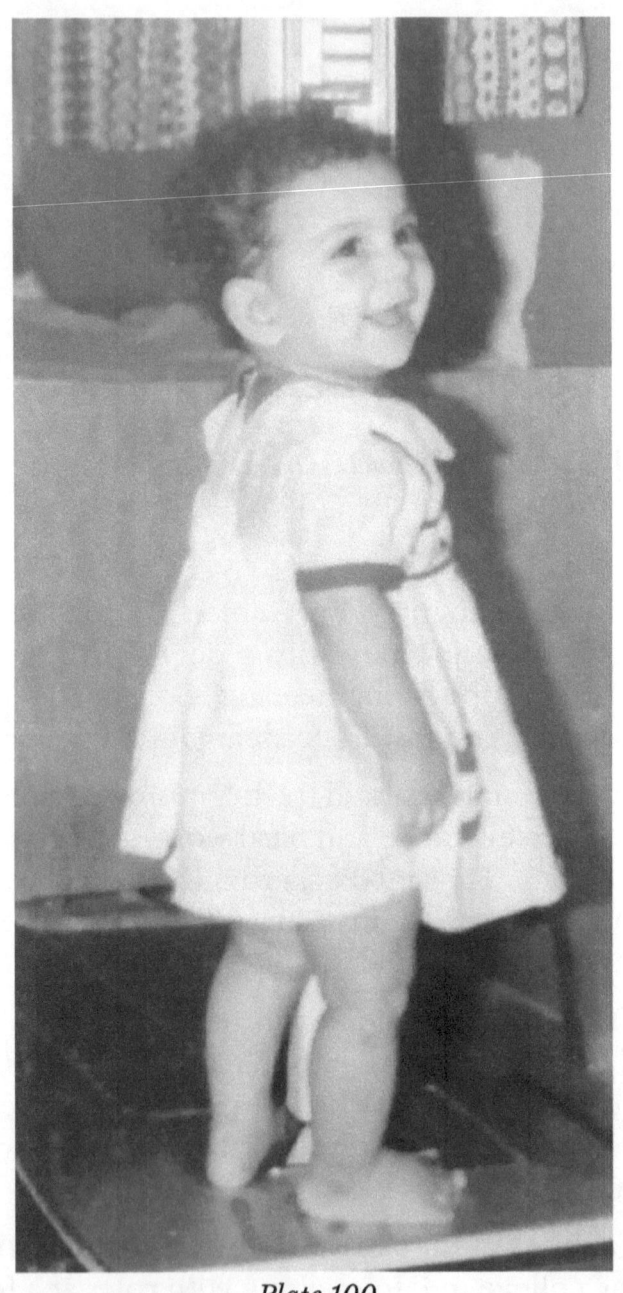

Plate 100
Our younger daughter, Gunjan Sharma. Clicked in Nigeria, 1986

persistence paid off when she found her niche at Appirio, which was later acquired by WIPRO, one of the leading global IT companies.

For over a decade, Gunjan has been a key player at WIPRO, rising to the position of Global Head, Quality Assurance and Business Analysis for the WIPRO Salesforce Practice. This remarkable achievement underscores her capabilities and dedication.

In her childhood, we often used to say on a lighter note that she was neither as naturally intelligent as her elder sister nor as hardworking as her brother. However, her success speaks volumes about her abilities.

Gunjan's decade-long tenure at WIPRO's Jaipur office highlights her commitment and achievements. She continues to excel professionally while balancing her family and community responsibilities. Her career has also taken her around the globe, including two short assignments in the United States, demonstrating her versatility and expertise.

> *"Life's challenges are not supposed to paralyse you; they're supposed to help you discover who you are."*
>
> *- Bernice Johnson Reagon*

I recall an incident during Gunjan's school days when I received a call from her teacher requesting a meeting. When I arrived, I was led to the principal's office, where concerns were raised about Gunjan struggling with science and mathematics. The suggestion was to consider switching her to commerce.

Despite these concerns, I was adamant that she should continue with science and mathematics if she desired so. I firmly told the principal, "She will manage with science and maths. Just guide her, but please don't change her subjects." As a result, her subjects remained unchanged.

Gunjan's passion for singing also stood out during her school years. She frequently expressed her desire to pursue singing seriously, but I encouraged her to prioritise her studies. These pivotal moments helped shape her future, as she learned to balance her academic pursuits with her personal interests. Today, her professional success is a testament to her hard work and determination.

Gunjan now lives in Jaipur with her two sons, Raghav and Parth. Her husband, Er. Sunil Sharma, is the Chief Manager at Indian Overseas Bank.

Plate 101
Cherishing family time, Gunjan with her husband, Er. Sunil Sharma, elder son Raghav and younger son Parth.

Chapter 19

The Heartbreaking Loss
of Our Son and the Aftermath

In June 2018, my son Ankur, accompanied by his family, returned to India due to UAE legal requirements. He had a new assignment lined up at MetLife in Dubai but had to remain in India while MetLife processed his work visa.

After a month of anticipation, he finally received his visa at the end of July and departed for Dubai on the 30th to join MetLife as an Insurance Manager. While Ankur settled into his new role, his family stayed in India, awaiting their own visas.

My elder brother, the late Prof. Mahesh Kumar Sharma's only son, Gaurav Sharma, had a passion for travel. He frequently visited Dubai and forged connections with many Indians residing there, often sharing accommodations and creating a home away from home.

On 20th August, 2018, Ankur, Gaurav, and two other friends decided to embark on a trip to Muscat. They planned to drive to Salalah in a Pajero SUV, with Ankur at the wheel. What was meant to be a simple journey filled with laughter and camaraderie turned into a tragic ordeal.

At approximately 6:30 p.m., about 20 km beyond Haima, their vehicle collided head-on with another car coming from the opposite direction. The collision was severe, causing both vehicles to catch fire immediately. The doors were jammed, trapping all six passengers inside. In a matter of moments, lives were lost.

The police investigation later revealed that the other car was at fault. The driver, travelling at high speed, lost control, leading to the catastrophic collision. As the Royal Oman Police had been tracing the details of the deceased ones, after two days, on 22nd August, we received the heartbreaking news from my nephew Mr. Pranay Sharma and our daughter-in-law's brother Mr. Anurag Vyas that the accident was fatal and there was no survivor. I was meditating (Vipassana) in our basement and was called upstairs where my elder daughter delivered the tragic news to me and my wife. Family members gradually gathered. I remained calm and composed amidst the sorrow.

The news of the accident had shattered our world. Losing Ankur, my beloved son, in such a sudden and violent manner was a pain beyond words. The void left by Ankur's untimely death is immense. He was more than just a son; he was a beacon of hope and joy in our lives. His laughter, his dreams and his zest for life were extinguished in an instant, leaving us grappling with the heavy silence of his absence. The memories of that fateful day haunt us, a constant reminder of life's fragility and fate's unpredictability.

Plate 102
My son Ankur and nephew Gaurav's last shared picture of good times in Dubai. A few days later, we lost them in a tragic accident in Oman. (Ankur sitting on right side and Gaurav on left)

Bringing Ankur & Gaurav back to India after 15 days of their Demise: The Journey of Grief and Endurance

Bringing Ankur and Gaurav to India after their demise required significant effort. We learned that the bodies were burnt and charred beyond recognition, necessitating a DNA test to identify them, for which blood relatives were to reach Muscat.

On 24th August, my nephew Tanmay (Gaurav's son), who was nine years old, my younger brother Subhash, who had lived in Oman for over a decade, and I flew to Muscat to identify our loved ones. Blood samples were collected and sent to the Department of Forensic Medicine and Mortuary at the Royal Oman Police Hospital. In the meantime, we requested the police to just show the bodies but they showed us only after the DNA test reports were ready.

The repatriation process involved coordination between the police, the Indian Embassy and Air India. The embassy had appointed Mr. Shameer Pookaparath Thazha Kuniyil, an Indian (likely from Kerala), to assist us with post-death formalities. He was immensely helpful in arranging lodging, boarding, and local transport. He also facilitated the embalming, sealing, and airlifting of the bodies. We remain profoundly grateful for Mr. Shameer's assistance, as he went out of his way to support us during this difficult time.

On 2nd September, we left Muscat and arrived in Delhi on the morning of 3rd September. It took nearly three hours to complete all formalities at the airport. Throughout the ordeal, we maintained constant communication with our family in Jaipur and my in-laws in Delhi. Preparations were made for Ankur and Gaurav's arrival, including arranging a large ambulance at the airport.

We finally left Delhi airport with two coffins in the ambulance. Accompanied by my nephew Tanmay and my brother Subhash, we began the sorrowful journey back to Jaipur. It was a heavy journey with grief and disbelief. At around 2 p.m., we reached our residence after 11 days. The local market was closed, reflecting the community's respect and mourning. Over a hundred people had gathered, their faces mirroring the collective grief. Preparations for the cremation were already in place.

For the final 'darshan', we allowed only the top 1-2 feet of their heads to be visible. The priest performed the last rites and rituals, and within half an hour, the two biers were prepared and taken to the cremation ground.

News of the tragic accident had spread widely, with local newspapers covering the story, including photographs of Ankur, Gaurav, and the burning cars. The scene at the cremation ground was indescribable.

As the procession moved toward the cremation site, people stepped out of their shops to witness the two biers side by side. They prayed for the departed souls, and passersby offered silent condolences. The community's support and shared grief provided a small measure of comfort during this devastating time. At the cremation ground, over a hundred people awaited our arrival, the atmosphere heavy with emotion as the mortal remains were placed on pyres side by side.

The memory of that day, the profound sense of loss, and the final journey of Ankur and Gaurav will forever be etched in our hearts. It was a day marked by sorrow, but also by the love and solidarity of those who stood by us in our darkest hour.

So, this is how our two children were cremated after 15 days of their death, on 3rd of September, 2018. The day of their cremation was also 'Janmashtami', a day typically celebrated with joy and devotion, but for us, it was marked by deep sorrow and loss. The contrast between the festive occasion and our personal tragedy added another layer of poignancy to the farewell.

Navigating the International Bureaucracy After Ankur's Demise

In 2019, I faced the monumental task of handling legal and bureaucratic formalities after Ankur left us. My nephew Pranay highlighted the logistical challenges of managing everything from India. Incidentally, my younger brother Subhash, Pranay's father, was in Dubai for two months. He strongly emphasised that my presence was crucial for completing the necessary tasks. Recognizing the gravity of the situation, I prepared for the journey.

On 2nd December, I arrived in Dubai, overwhelmed by a wave of emotions as I confronted the memories of happier times spent there. I braced myself for the bureaucratic process, which was long and intricate. Every document required verification by Indian agencies, attestation, and translation into Arabic, leading to numerous visits to various offices.

The process was interlinked: for instance, the car insurance claim could not be processed until the car loan from Dubai Islamic Bank was cleared. I settled the loan in cash, obtained a certificate, and proceeded with the insurance claim. The bureaucratic demands were daunting, but I progressed step by step.

Each morning, my nephew dropped my brother and me off at either the bank or court. The court routine was exhaustive, involving extensive document verification, translation, and submission. Over time, we became familiar faces, with court staff occasionally assisting us to expedite the process. Despite the emotional and physical toll, moments of kindness from the staff provided some solace. Despite the obstacles, we made steady progress. Subhash stood by me through the entire process. His company gave me a lot of strength and made even difficult tasks look manageable.

By February, Subhash's visa was nearing expiration, and he had to return to India. I continued the work, supported by Pranay, navigating the daily routine of handling court documents, visiting banks, and meetings with insurance representatives. The tasks demanded constant attention and unwavering persistence.

By March, I had nearly completed all formalities, but my visa was also close to expiring. A contact at a money exchange helped transfer the remaining funds, which was a significant relief. I finalised the financial matters just in time and returned to India on 2nd March, 2020. The COVID-19 pandemic was beginning to spread, creating a tense atmosphere upon my arrival. Shortly thereafter, the Indian government imposed a complete lockdown, adding further complexity to the situation.

Reflecting on my experience in Dubai, it was a period marked by emotional and physical exhaustion. The bureaucratic hurdles were significant, and the process was often daunting, but the support from my family and unexpected kindness from strangers helped me navigate through the challenges. This journey, though arduous, highlighted the importance of perseverance and the strength of familial bonds in times of adversity.

The tasks completed in Dubai were not just about fulfilling legal obligations; they were about honouring Ankur's memory and ensuring that his affairs were settled with dignity and respect. This experience underscored the resilience needed to navigate life's most challenging moments and the importance of support and solidarity from loved ones.

Chapter 20

From Chaos to Clarity: Spiritual Metamorphosis with Vipassana

The technique that transformed my life entirely was Vipassana meditation. This was a major turning point in my life. Although I have never been greedy, envious or dishonest, as my father had instilled the traits of honesty, hard work, contentment and optimism in me, retrospectively I realise that before discovering Vipassana, I had ego and anger issues. These traits were significant weaknesses that dominated my personality, causing strain in my relationships and turmoil within myself.

When we finally returned to India from Nigeria in 1988, it felt like a homecoming after a long journey. In 1989, I joined the Agricultural Research Station in Fatehpur Shekhawati. My journey towards discovering Vipassana began through a dear friend, Mr. Ashok Chauhan. Mr. Chauhan's father, Mr. Ram Singhji, held the prestigious position of Home Secretary in the Rajasthan government. As an IAS officer, Mr. Ram Singhji was a man of great influence and wisdom. He had learned Vipassana from Shri

S.N. Goenkaji, who had reintroduced this ancient practice to India.

However, the seed of curiosity was planted in my mind in 1990 when Mr. Chauhan introduced me to the technique, but I could not attend it until 2007 because I assumed a 10 day leave at a stretch would not be possible, being in service. After retirement, I immediately contacted Mr. Ashok Chauhan and expressed my desire to attend a Vipassana course. Mr.Chauhan would often speak about how Vipassana had transformed his family's life. His father's serene demeanour and balanced approach to life were testaments to the profound impact of this meditation practice. Intrigued by their experiences, I felt a strong pull towards understanding what Vipassana was all about.

Mr. Ram Singhji, inspired by Shri Goenkaji's teachings, adopted Vipassana and instilled its values in his family. Mr.Chauhan's narratives about their family retreats and the peace they had found through Vipassana piqued my curiosity further. He described how Goenka Ji had started conducting 10-day courses across India, teaching the practice in temples, churches, mosques, and other communal spaces. Despite his initial concerns about acceptance, the technique's profound impact began attracting many individuals of different communities seeking inner peace.

Hearing these stories, I felt an urge to explore Vipassana myself. It was clear that this was more than just a meditation technique; it was a way of life that brought harmony, clarity, and self-realisation. The influence it had on Mr.Chauhan's family, particularly on his father, was undeniable.

> *"Vipassana meditation is the key to unlock the door to self-awareness and inner peace."*

Mr. Ashok explained to me that Vipassana, which means "to see things as they really are," was a technique rediscovered by Lord Buddha over 2,600 years ago. However, the practice had almost vanished from India and had been preserved in Burma in its pristine form. The Goenka family, who had settled in Burma three generations ago, became the custodians of this valuable tradition. Shri S.N. Goenkaji, trained by the Burmese teacher Sayagyi U Ba Khin, decided to bring this practice back to India in 1969.

The Goenka family came into contact with Burmese teachers who had maintained this tradition with unwavering dedication. Each Burmese teacher took it upon themselves to train at least one disciple to carry forward the practice. One such teacher was Sayagyi U Ba Khin, who trained Shri S.N. Goenkaji, a Burmese-Indian businessman.

Shri S.N. Goenkaji returned to India in 1969, bringing with him the invaluable practice of Vipassana. Goenka Ji's approach was unique. He was not a monk. He travelled with his wife Smt, Elaichi Devi Goenka (Mataji), maintaining his household life. His relatable persona and the profound impact of Vipassana led to its widespread acceptance.

Eventually, a dedicated centre was established in Igatpuri, Nasik district, where the practice was taught in its purest form. This centre became a sanctuary for those seeking inner peace and self-realisation. Vipassana spread globally under the guidance of Shri S.N. Goenkaji. Today, there are international centres worldwide. At every centre, the code of discipline, time table etc. are identical. In Jaipur too we have a beautiful centre.

"In the quiet of meditation, we find the strength to overcome our deepest fears and embrace our true selves."

The essence of Vipassana lies in its rigorous 10-day camp, where noble silence is observed. Participants are not allowed to speak or communicate in any way. Mobile phones are deposited upon arrival, and any necessary communication is done through teachers or servers, ensuring complete focus on the practice.

Discovering Vipassana was a turning point in my life. It helped me overcome my weaknesses and transformed me into a calmer, more balanced person. The anger that once consumed me was replaced with serenity. The ego that overshadowed my relationships was replaced with humility. There was a deep sense of contentment.

Vipassana taught me to observe my thoughts and emotions without reacting to them. It gave me the tools to understand myself better and to make peace with my inner turmoil. The journey through Vipassana is profound, and its benefits are immeasurable, touching every aspect of life. It is a path to liberation, a journey towards self-discovery, and a profound realisation of the interconnectedness of all beings.

I learned that there is a centre in Jaipur also, which is said to be the second-largest and second oldest Vipassana centre in the world, known as 'Dhamma Thali'. The largest is in Igatpuri, Nasik district, Maharashtra. These centres offer the courses free of charge, including accommodation and meals, though donations are welcome if participants wish to contribute (only after they have done atleast one course free of cost initially). Gautam Buddha had emphasised that if Dharma (the teachings) were turned into a commercial commodity, its true essence would be lost.

Commercialization would lead to ego inflation and monetary considerations overshadowing the spiritual essence. Thus, the courses were kept free to preserve their purity.

My First 10 day Vipassana Course

In 2007, I attended my first ten-day course at 'Dhamma Thali' from 11th to 22nd September. It is a beautiful centre nestled in the lap of nature, surrounded by mountains and greenery, attracting many foreign visitors too.

Initially, I was very ignorant about the technique. The evening discourses, delivered through audio-video format by Shri S.N. Goenkaji (Guruji), were enlightening. The assistant teachers present to guide us were compassionate and understanding. Though I didn't grasp everything during those ten days, a seed was sown within me. By the end of the course, I realised that Vipassana was the only way to live a peaceful life. This was the only path, which could reduce suffering and lead to liberation in a true sense.

The journey through this 10-day Vipassana camp was a transformative experience, and I can personally attest to its profound impact. As I immersed myself in the process, I discovered the intricate workings of the mind and body and the path to inner peace and wisdom. Each evening, we attended discourses that explained the day's practice and the reasons behind it. The insights shared during these discourses were profound and enlightening.

Plate 103
Entrance Gate of Dhamma Thali, the Vipassana Centre in Jaipur. It is the second largest and the second oldest Vipassana Centre in the world.

Vipassana began to address my deep-seated issues of anger and ego. It became clear that these emotions were the sources of my suffering. With continued practice, I noticed only a very minimal reduction in these negativities, still it was a significant breakthrough for me. Understanding that these emotions led to suffering was the first step towards transformation.

Understanding The Technique of Vipassana: The Path to Inner Peace

Vipassana, a technique rediscovered by Lord Buddha, is rooted in the eightfold Path, which is a guideline for ethical and mental development. This path is divided into three main sections: Sīla (morality), Samādhi (concentration of mind), and Paññā (wisdom – purification of mind).

Sila represents the moral principles essential for leading a virtuous life. It comprises five key principles: refraining from lying, abstaining from killing any living being, avoiding theft, practising chastity and fidelity, and steering clear of intoxicants. These moral guidelines form the bedrock of a disciplined life, helping ensure that our actions do not cause harm to others or ourselves.

Samadhi involves mastering the mind, which often drifts between past regrets and future anxieties, rarely staying in the present. To develop concentration, one must learn to focus the mind. Vipassana offers a unique approach that is free from religious or sectarian bias. Instead of relying on external objects of focus, such as images, mantras, or deities, Vipassana centres on the breath. The breath is a universal, natural, and neutral object of attention. This practice, known as Ānāpānasati, involves simply observing the breath as it flows in and out. While the technique is straightforward, it can be challenging. Initially, it may be difficult to maintain continuous awareness of the breath for even a few seconds, as the mind tends to wander. However, with consistent practice, one can train the mind to remain focused and calm, which is essential for deeper meditation.

The Story of the Child and the Mother

Imagine a young child playing outside in the mud, getting thoroughly dirty. When he comes back inside, his mother repeatedly tells him to sit under the faucet so she can clean him. However, the child keeps getting up and running away, over and over again. How can she clean him if he won't stay still?

- **The Child as Our Mind** - This story serves as a powerful metaphor for our own minds. The child represents our mind, which is often restless, filled with a mix of good and bad thoughts and habits. Just like the child who needs to sit still to be cleaned, our mind needs to become stable and focused to be purified and cleansed of its impurities.

- **Stability Before Cleansing** - In the practice of Vipassana, this stability is achieved through the first two steps of Sīla (morality) and Samādhi (concentration). These steps help our mind to settle, creating the necessary stillness. Only when the mind is stable can we proceed to the next step, Paññā (wisdom) - where deep purification happens.

Paññā, or wisdom, represents the third and final stage of the Vipassana technique, where profound insight into the nature of reality is attained. Traditionally, this stage was not taught openly but was instead experienced directly through practice.

During the **Paññā** practice, meditators closely observe bodily sensations. This requires a highly focused and refined mind, which is developed through the earlier practice of Ānāpānasati (awareness of breathing).

Application of Vipassana in Daily Life

Let me explain Gautam Buddha's discovered technique and how it fundamentally changed my understanding of reactions and emotions. As one goes through daily life, external stimuli, be it praise or criticism, trigger various sensations in the body. These sensations can lead to reactions such as craving or aversion. In Hindi, these reactions are known as 'Raag' (attachment) and 'Dwesh' (aversion). Both these reactions are considered detrimental because they disrupt the mind's equilibrium.

Imagine someone talks to you in an insulting way. Naturally, you feel angry. However, the anger isn't directly caused by the insult. Instead, it arises because of the way your mind reacts when it perceives the words of insult. This reaction triggers a biochemical response in your body, releasing certain hormones. The insult itself isn't the direct cause of your anger; it's your mind's conditioned reaction to it, based on your past experiences, expectations and belief systems. Every time we react to something, be it positive or negative, our body experiences various sensations. These sensations of either attachment or aversion are sources of suffering.

Buddha taught the Middle Path, avoiding both extreme self-indulgence and extreme self mortification. This path involves understanding and observing the nature of our sensations without reacting to them. In Vipassana, the key is to observe these sensations **(sajagta)** with a balanced and equanimous mind **(samta)**. By doing so, one realises that these sensations are temporary **(anicca)** and will fade away with time. This realisation helps in breaking the cycle of reaction and fosters a state of inner peace.

> *"Vipassana is a journey of self-transformation through self observation"*
>
> *– Buddh Vipassana Meditation*

Progress on the Path of Vipassana

I continued attending courses, progressing to 20-day and even 30-day courses. In Hyderabad, I reserved a spot for my first 45 day course from 31st May to 15th July, 2023, but due to medical reasons could not attend it. Coincidentally, these were the exact 45 days when I underwent radiation therapy.

From my first course in September 2007, to the forty-two courses I have completed since then, Vipassana has been a cornerstone of my life. Out of these, four were attended in Dubai, with the rest in India. I have been regularly practising Vipassana even at home for two hours daily for the last 17 years.

Looking back, I can testify that Vipassana was the light that guided me out of the darkness. It was the anchor that steadied me through life's storms. It was the key that unlocked a deeper understanding of myself and the world around me. For this, I am eternally grateful. This journey has been the major turning point of my life. The practice of Vipassana has brought profound peace and understanding, allowing me to live a more harmonious life. It has been a transformative experience, reshaping my approach to life's challenges and helping me cultivate a sense of inner tranquillity.

After experiencing the benefits myself, I had a feeling of *'maîtri'* (good wishes and compassion) for all beings. I told others in my family and encouraged them to attend a course, with a feeling that each and everyone should be liberated from their sufferings and should walk on a path leading to peace and happiness. My wife, elder sister, younger brother's wife, youngest brother and his wife, my elder daughter, her mother- law, my son, my nephew, niece and her daughter too, all have attended at least one 10 day Vipassana course and have been benefited. Although regular practice benefits more, yes attending at least one 10 day course is the first step on this path.

Serving as a Volunteer

Throughout my journey, I also served as a volunteer, assisting meditators with any problems they faced during the courses. This involved managing logistics, providing support, and ensuring that the participants had a smooth experience. Serving in these courses allowed me to understand the challenges that meditators encounter, particularly during the 10-day course, where new meditators also join the old ones.

Mr Anil Mehtaji, a Vipassana teacher, offered me to take the responsibility as a teacher too. This was a great honour for me, but due to my personal, family and health related limitations, and a bit of travelling too which was required, I could not take up this responsibility.

My Aspirations to Travel to the Four Significant Buddhist Places

As a devoted practitioner of Vipassana and an admirer of Buddha's teachings, there are four places I deeply wish to visit and meditate there. Each of these places holds immense historical and spiritual significance, reflecting key moments in the life of Gautama Buddha.

Lumbini, Nepal: The Birthplace of Buddha

Bodh Gaya: The Site of Enlightenment (Nirvana)

Sarnath: The First Sermon (Dharma Chakra Pravartan)

Kushinagar: Mahaparinirvana

Significance of Buddha Purnima

The full moon night in the Vaisakh month of Hindu calendar (falling in either April or May months) is known as the Buddha Purnima. It has a spiritual and religious importance. This day marks the three most significant events in Lord Buddha's life, his birth, attainment of enlightenment and Mahaparinirvana (death). On this day, special meditation group sittings are arranged at Vipassana centres across the world. I have been fortunate enough to have attended many of such sittings at Dhamma Thali with my family. The atmosphere is serene and peaceful, it's an altogether different experience, meditating together under the full moon.

Plate 104
After a group meditation at Dhamma Thali on the occasion of Buddha Purnima, 23rd May, 2024

Strength from Vipassana during the darkest days of life: My own experiences

With a deeper understanding of the technique, through long courses covering 20 and 30 days, and regular morning-evening practice for the last 17 years, I got a chance to experience the positive impact of the technique in my life.

During my son's demise, after completing the rites and rituals, I started settling down and in the next seven months, I went to Dhamma thali and attended six courses, out of which, in three I served as a Dhamma server. This helped me to assess myself about the depth of the technique further.

Since the diagnosis of my cancer, it's been a journey of more than a year now, with the treatment still continuing. However, I have been able to cope up without much mental trauma in spite of the surgeries and radiation involved. I owe this strength, equanimity and peace to Vipassana meditation.

Chapter 21

Defying the Odds: My Relentless Fight Against Cancer

One of my most profound experiences occurred during a course I attended from 28th March to 3rd April, 2023, at the Dhamma Thali, the Vipassana Centre in Jaipur. This course was special because it focused on the teachings of Gautama Buddha on how to practise Vipassana. The course, known as the 'Satipatthana Course', was designed to last for eight days, and I started it with great enthusiasm.

The first few days proceeded normally without any significant incident. However, on the evening of 3rd April, something unexpected happened. At around 5:40 PM, while I was relaxing in my room and preparing to head to the meditation hall for group sitting, I experienced a sudden disorientation. It was as if I lost all sense of direction and time, a condition known as 'Disha Bhram'. I wasn't unconscious, but I was completely disoriented and confused.

When the volunteers, who regularly check on participants, noticed my absence, they came to my room. I had bolted the door from inside and did not respond to their calls. Sensing something unusual, they decided to break the door. In my disoriented state, I was unable to comprehend what was happening.

So on the evening of 3rd April, 2023, around 6 PM, my family received a call from the volunteers of that camp. Despite feeling an unsettling sense of disorientation, I managed to speak and reassure my daughter on the phone, "Yes, everything is fine beta." A strange, unexplainable sensation clouded my thoughts.

Medical Emergency Amidst the Protest

This was a challenging time. The Right to Health Bill (RTH) had just been passed by the Ashok Gehlot government, leading to a widespread protest among the medical community. Hospitals were shut down and only a few emergency services were operational. Over a lakh doctors were on the streets protesting against the flawed clauses of the RTH Bill. Amidst this chaos, my condition added another layer of complexity and urgency.

The Decision to Go to Manipal Hospital

Given the dire situation, my son-in-law, the head of critical care medicine, decided that we had no choice but to go to Manipal Hospital. His decisive action brought a glimmer of hope in a sea of uncertainty. He called the hospital, and an ambulance was dispatched to our home. My son-in-law and elder daughter also rushed to my house. I was brought from the Vipassana centre to our house in a car accompanied by Anil Mehtaji and one more person from the centre. The ambulance sent from Manipal was well-equipped, as they were unsure about my exact condition. All the three vehicles reached almost simultaneously at my residence.

My wife, daughter, son in law and brother Kailash all received me. Although I seemed disoriented, I tried to smile and interact with them. I was lying in the back seat of the car and was immediately shifted to the ambulance waiting there. Despite my drowsiness and altered sensorium, I remained composed and peaceful, likely due to the strength Vipassana had given me. I clung to this inner calm, even as my body betrayed me.

In the ambulance, I was immediately taken to the critical care unit of Manipal hospital. Upon reaching Manipal Hospital, a CT scan revealed a subdural haemorrhage (bleeding between the brain and its coverings), explaining my altered sensorium. The diagnosis was a shock, yet it brought clarity. I was placed under conservative management, but the journey was far from over.

The Diagnosis of a Rare Malignancy (Cancer)

The following morning, a vigilant radiologist, Dr Manoj, noticed a suspicious lesion on my skull during a review of the scans. I had a cyst on my head for the past eight or nine years, which had slightly increased in size over the last two to three years. Despite regular health check-ups, the cyst had not been further evaluated as it was considered benign (non cancerous).

Further evaluation this time revealed a cancerous growth in the cyst, which had spread to the skull bone. The biopsy was taken from the suspected lymph nodes and it was found to be a rare kind of cancer '**Adenoid Cystic Carcinoma Of Scalp**'.

But through the haze of fear and uncertainty, I found a profound sense of peace and acceptance. This inner calm, nurtured through years of practice of Vipassana, became my anchor in the storm.

The Nine Hours Long Surgery at Mahatma Gandhi Hospital

I don't remember anything about being taken to the hospital. One moment, I was disoriented in my room at the Vipassana Centre; the next, I found myself in a hospital bed. The transition was a blur. Thereafter, I spent about seven to eight days in Manipal hospital before being transferred to Mahatma Gandhi Medical College and Hospital.

The decision to shift me to Mahatma Gandhi Medical College and Hospital was crucial. Fortunately, Dr. Bhawani Shankar Sharma, a renowned name in the medical field and a retired Head of Department of Neurosurgery, from AIIMS Delhi, was working there at the time. His expertise was invaluable to my treatment. I was transferred to this facility for the required surgery and more specialised treatment under him.

First time, I was operated on 12th April, 2023. The surgery was extensive, lasting approximately nine hours. A skilled team of surgeons, including Dr B.S. Sharma, the neurosurgeon and Dr. Dinesh Yadav, an oncosurgeon (my daughter's and son in law's MBBS batchmate) operated. They were joined by a plastic surgeon who handled the reconstruction of the resected scalp part and experienced anaesthetists who ensured everything went smoothly.

The surgery was complex and meticulous. A significant portion of the bone was removed, along with all the blood clots and the tumour mass. The surgeons also removed lymph nodes from my neck, as they were found to be positive for malignancy (cancer). During the operation, a team of pathologists examined the tissue in real-time, determining the extent of the cancer and ensuring all affected tissues were removed. If the margins of the resected tissue were positive, they would continue resecting until they were confident that no cancerous tissue remained.

After the surgery, a graft was taken from my thigh to reconstruct the removed scalp part. This procedure required careful monitoring and frequent dressings. The road to recovery was long and challenging, but I remained hopeful and determined. The graft was not healing due to the disturbed blood supply subsequent to the major surgical resection.

The Rejection of Skin Graft, Delaying the Radiation Therapy

After the surgery at Mahatma Gandhi Hospital, I was discharged to home on oral medications with advice for regular dressing of surgical sites. The plan was radiation therapy further, once the stitches and the graft healed.

Despite regular and meticulous dressings, the split skin graft at my scalp got necrosed (rejected) and the planned radiotherapy got delayed for the time being, as it could only be started after the healing of the graft.

The Second Graft Surgery Planned, but Cancelled: Development of Deep Vein Thrombosis (DVT), another Medical Emergency

We took advice at Bhagwan Mahaveer Cancer Hospital & Research Centre (BMCHRC), where our radiation therapy was planned in near future. This time a different type of skin graft, a free flap graft was suggested. In this a thicker skin graft from the thigh was to be taken along with its blood supply, and was to be placed on the scalp with vascular repair there.

I got admitted at BMCHRC on 1st May and the surgery was scheduled for 2nd May. However, on the 2nd May morning, I noticed significant swelling on my left leg which was extending upto my thigh and my leg was swollen and as hard as a watermelon.

Meanwhile we got a call from the OT to be shifted for the surgery, but my son in law suspected it to be 'Deep Vein Thrombosis (DVT)', which was confirmed there by doppler ultrasound. I was told that this condition carries a risk of pulmonary embolism (clot of leg vein going to Lung's circulation), which can be a life threatening condition. Thus the repeat graft surgery was postponed.

Back to Manipal; Anticoagulation Therapy (Blood thinners): The Double Edged Sword in My Case

I was started on anticoagulant injections and was again shifted to Manipal Hospital so that we could avail better multispeciality care including interventional cardiology support, in case required.

There at Manipal Hospital, I was again admitted for seven days ,being kept on anticoagulation injections with close neurological monitoring as it was a double edged sword in my case. The anticoagulation treatment could have caused brain haemorrhage again, as it had occurred earlier too and moreover, now I was a post neurosurgery patient also. On the other hand, it was essential too in view of DVT, to prevent further life threatening complications.

During my stay at Manipal Hospital I found that the ICU staff were very kind and compassionate. Initially I thought it was because of my son in law but later I realised that they were equally good to other patients as well. My stay at Manipal even with so much of uncertainties and health issues remains memorable due to those smiling faces. God bless them all.

The Second Graft Surgery (Free Flap): An Important Decision Amidst the Complexities

After stabilisation, we decided to proceed with the pending free flap (graft) surgery. My son in law discussed the whole case with a young plastic surgeon having a gifted surgical hand at Mahatma Gandhi Hospital, Dr Manish Jain. He understood the complexity, that surgery with therapeutic anticoagulation going on could lead to bleeding and a graft rejection again. He also understood that the anticoagulation could not be stopped as recently there had been Deep vein thrombosis. Adding to the complexity, without the repeat surgery of graft, the pending radiation therapy could not be started. He was confident enough and told us that he will perform the surgery even with full anticoagulation.

Finally, I was operated on at Mahatma Gandhi hospital for the second time on 12th May, 2023, exactly one month after my first surgery there itself. I remember my daughter, Sangita, waving to me as I was being taken inside the operation theatre (OT) on a trolley. The doctors and staff were pleased to see and appreciated how I smilingly waved back to her. They conveyed to Sangita that it was a rare scene for them to see someone with such calm, peace and strength, especially during a second surgery with the known diagnosis.

This was also a prolonged surgery, after which I was kept on a ventilator.

The Next Morning After the Surgery; The Cardiac Event (A Heart Attack)

Throughout the day and night, and yet the next morning, my son in law, Dr.Vaibhav was there with me in the ICU. The next morning, while I was still on the ventilator, he informed me that we were going to 'Cath Lab' (cardiology lab) for angiography. I had a cardiac event, a heart attack, which was managed conservatively. Next day, they removed my ventilator and after a stay of seven more days, I was discharged from the hospital.

Dressing on my thigh continued for a long period because there was continuous oozing of blood from the surgical sites, both on head and the left thigh, due to the ongoing anticoagulation treatment. It took about two and a half months for my thigh wound to heal completely. Every alternate day, dressing was done at my home by my son in law, with review from surgeons in between.

At Last the Radiation Therapy Began

In the meanwhile, under the compassionate care and able guidance of Dr Tej Prakash Soni (another MBBS batchmate of my daughter and son in law), my radiation therapy sessions started from 31st May, 2023 at Bhagwan Mahaveer Cancer Hospital and Research Centre. We were able to start the radiation therapy just within the desired time limit after the initial surgery. 36 sessions were executed from 31st May to 15th July, the exact 45 days for which I had booked a slot earlier for my first 45 day Vipassana Meditation course in Hyderabad, but had to cancel due to obvious reasons later.

The Follow up PET Scan: A Short Duration of Big Relief

In September 2023, I underwent a routine PET scan and MRI. Both tests came back normal, which was a relief. The doctors recommended repeating the scans after six months to monitor my condition closely.

The Recurrence; the Dilemma; the Second Course of Radiation Therapy

On 3rd April, 2024, I had another PET Scan. This time, the scan revealed a concerning development: a layer of suspicious lesions covering my brain (meningeal metastasis). The doctors suggested a second round of radiation therapy, but this time, it would be whole-brain radiation. The news was unsettling, but I steeled myself for the upcoming treatment, hoping for the best outcome. It was during these sessions, I agreed to my elder daughter's hesitant request of starting the narrations for this book. The doctors told me that I might develop forgetfulness and become dull and drowsy. But somehow I managed and the sessions completed.

After the 10 whole-brain radiation sessions in April, 2024, we began exploring further options. We consulted with a lot of people to determine if there was any role for further chemotherapy or immunotherapy. The decision was complex and needed careful consideration. We sought teleconsultations from renowned institutions like Tata Memorial Hospital, Mumbai. Samples taken for biopsy were sent to the USA. The expertise and advice from these consultations were invaluable as we navigated through the uncertainties of my treatment plan. From May 10 onwards, as suggested by Dr Deepak Shukla, a brilliant oncologist in Manipal Hospital, we have started metronomic chemotherapy, in a daily dose of one capsule.

Plate 105
With my daughters, Sangita (on left) and Gunjan (on right), December, 2023

Near Complete Resolution (Regression): A New Ray of Hope

It was decided to repeat the PET scan after three months to see if the disease is progressing or if it has become static. The follow up PET scan and MRI on 5th August, 2024 revealed near complete resolution (regression) of the layer of dural metastases around the brain, which was the matter of great concern on the previous scan. Although small lesions on two vertebrae are still there, their size remains static. The oral chemotherapy continues, along with my journey of fortitude and hope.

"The storms of life may rage, but an indomitable spirit remains steadfast and unyielding."

The journey was challenging, but the continuous support and guidance from the medical community provided a beacon of hope. This entire experience, from the initial disorientation to the extensive surgery, two rounds of radiation therapy and partial recovery, has been a testament to the fragility and resilience of life. The medical team's expertise and the support of my family were instrumental in navigating this journey. Throughout this ordeal, the practice of Vipassana meditation provided me with an inner strength and peace that carried me through the darkest moments of my life. This journey, though arduous, has deepened my appreciation for life and the incredible resilience of the human spirit.

My Near-Death Experience

When I had my near-death experience, being on a ventilator after the second surgery, I was not at all disturbed. It was an intense moment, and I initially hesitated to share it, but eventually, I opened up to my son-in-law, daughter, and wife later.

The doctors frequently checked on me, opening my eyes, and examining me with a torch. I was aware of everything happening around me and could hear them clearly. I could understand everything but since I was completely paralyzed, I could neither move my hands nor my legs, not even a millimetre. I felt utterly immobilised.

During this time, my son-in-law also told me that my grandson, Prabhav, had scored 97% in his 10th board exams, something I had asked about daily. This was a piece of news that brought me immense joy, even though I couldn't move a muscle to express it.

I felt like my last moments were approaching as the doctors kept checking my eyes frequently. Strangely, I felt a sense of happiness and peace rather than fear or sadness. I even imagined being taken away from my bed and experienced a few jolts. My son-in-law later told me that they had taken me for an angiography on a trolley in a lift.

At one point, I thought they were about to give me a final injection of adrenaline, straight into my heart. I imagined the final moments, thinking they would inform my family and prepare for my body's return home.

The Unwavering Support:

During my entire treatment and hospitalisation, my wife single handedly took care of most of the household tasks including arranging medicines and other essentials, for which I am incredibly grateful.

I would like to make a special mention of my younger brother, Dr. Subhash. He played a crucial role in coordinating everything along with my son in law

Dr.Vaibhav, ensuring that I received the best care in different hospitals. Despite being over seventy years of age, he demonstrated incredible energy and support, much like 'Lakshman for Ram'. I recall that he himself met with an accident while on his way to visit me at the hospital. Despite this, after receiving first aid and taking some medication, he continued to come and see me. I am immensely thankful for his presence and support during these challenging times.

> *"Even amidst the greatest trials, a resilient*
> *heart finds a way to rise and overcome."*

Despite all these developments, I have no regrets or dejection in my life. It has been more than a year now since I was diagnosed with Cancer. Since then, the treatment is ongoing without much mental or physical trauma. This has been made possible by Vipassana meditation.

Chapter 22

Dreams Unfolding: The Art of Finding Contentment and Peace in Simplicity

As I look towards the future, I find that I have no grand aspirations or lofty goals. I am truly happy and content with my life as it is. Many people wonder how I manage to remain so calm and balanced, even in the face of challenging situations such as my son's fatal accident and my own battle with cancer. The key to this calmness lies in my ability to stay composed and centred.

I spend my days with a simple yet profound aspiration: to wish well for everyone. I dedicate each day to sending out positive intentions for the well-being of all. I pray for everyone's happiness and for them to overcome their sorrows. This practice brings me immense peace and satisfaction.

I have no regrets about what I have achieved or what I have not. Regrets can create knots in our hearts, causing unnecessary sorrow and disturbance. By accepting everything that has happened, I am able to maintain a

Plate 106
A memory of Covid days, 1st June 2020

serene and joyful present. My present is beautiful, and I hope it continues to remain so.

> *"Adversity is the crucible in which true strength and resilience are forged."*
>
> *- Anonymous*

In essence, my future dreams are not about achieving more or reaching higher. They are about maintaining the tranquillity and contentment that I have found in my life. I wish for this simplicity and peace to continue, and I hope that others can find similar contentment in their own lives. This is my humble aspiration as I look ahead, embracing each moment with gratitude and serenity.

"Strength does not come from winning. Your struggles develop your strengths."

- Arnold Schwarzenegger

Epilogue

Reflections of a Life Lived with Optimism and Resilience

As I reflect on the journey of my life, it unfolds like a tapestry woven with threads of perseverance, joy, success, sorrow, resilience, hope and peace. From humble beginnings in a modest family to the bustling corridors of agricultural research at the prestigious Indian Agricultural Research Institute (IARI), universities of Germany & Nigeria, back to the countryside of Fatehpur and later the directorate in Bikaner, every step has been a testament to the power of perseverance and the unwavering support of loved ones.

My professional journey along with my passion to travel, led me to different places of the world, giving me an opportunity to explore different cultures and bond with people, which further enriched my experiences and knowledge.

Family has been the bedrock of my existence. The love and support of my wife, children, and extended family have been my anchor through turbulent seas and calm waters alike. Their unwavering belief in my dreams, coupled with their sacrifices and encouragement, have been the guiding force behind every achievement and every milestone.

Yet, life is not without its trials. The loss of my beloved son, Ankur, in a tragic accident in Oman shattered our world. The pain of that loss remains a constant ache in our hearts, a reminder of life's fragility and the importance of cherishing every moment with loved ones.

In facing my own battle with cancer, I confronted fear with fortitude and uncertainty with unwavering faith. The journey through illness taught me invaluable lessons about resilience, gratitude and the preciousness of life itself. It reinforced my belief in the indomitable human spirit and the transformative power of hope.

Central to my spiritual journey has been the practice of Vipassana meditation. Through its teachings of self-awareness and equanimity, I have found inner peace amidst life's storms, discovering a profound connection between mind, body, and spirit. Vipassana has not only deepened my understanding of human suffering but also strengthened my resolve to alleviate it through both medical science and compassionate care.

To those who walk alongside me on this journey, I offer these reflections: cherish your loved ones, nurture your dreams with unwavering determination and never underestimate the impact of a kind word or a helping hand. Life's greatest joys are found not in the grandeur of achievements, but in the quiet moments of connection and compassion.

*"As this story ends, I remain grateful for the life
I have lived, filled with simplicity, peace and contentment."*

– Dr. Trilok Raj Sharma

In closing, I am grateful for every twist and turn, every triumph and tribulation that has shaped the journey of my life. May my story serve as a beacon of hope for those navigating their own paths, a reminder that with courage, perseverance and love, we can overcome any obstacle and find fulfilment in the journey itself.

*Plate 107
Grateful for the life I've lived and the paths I've walked*

www.ingramcontent.com/pod-product-compliance
Lightning Source LLC
LaVergne TN
LVHW091625070526
838199LV00044B/948